MASTERS OF DECEPTION

MASTERS OF DECEPTION

A Christian Analysis of the Anti-Biblical Teachings of the Jehovah's Witnesses

F. W. THOMAS

BAKER BOOK HOUSE • GRAND RAPIDS, MICHIGAN

ISBN: 0-8010-8779-1

First printing, February 1972
Second printing, September 1973
Third printing, September 1974
Fourth printing, May 1976

PHOTOLITHOPRINTED BY CUSHING - MALLOY, INC.
ANN ARBOR, MICHIGAN, UNITED STATES OF AMERICA
1976

Dedication

This book is dedicated to the Lord God who miraculously spared the author from a watery grave. As a young man of twenty the writer joined the merchant marine. One day while having lifeboat drill in the midst of the Atlantic Ocean the following incident occurred.

I was at my station on the life boat deck waiting for orders from the captain to do my part in guiding the soon to be released lifeboat over the side. It so happened that I had to stand directly in the path that the lifeboat would swing into upon being released. It was necessary for me to take this position so that I could see the captain on the bridge. Upon his command I was to step out of the way and then take up a new position. While standing at my first station waiting for the captain's signal, suddenly a pair of strong but gentle hands grabbed me at the back of my knees knocking my legs out from under me. This caused me to fall firmly but gently to the deck of the ship. Immediately I turned to see the culprit who had just played this practical joke. To my utter amazement, there was no one at all near me! A few inches from where I now lay was the ship's edge and beyond this the open sea. (Cargo ships did not have railings on the lifeboat deck.) At the same instant, I suddenly became aware of the swish of the lifeboat *now swinging directly over my head!*

The lifeboat had apparently come loose prematurely. The men working on it were unable to notify the captain, and he consequently could not signal me to move out of the way in time. Had I not been grabbed by *unseen hands* and made to fall to the deck of the ship, I would have been hit by the swinging lifeboat, which probably weighed several thousand pounds, and knocked into the sea.

"Are you all right?" the captain shouted. Then he ordered me to the bridge, and exclaimed, "Man, you sure have tremendous reflexes! How did you know to fall just at that instant?" I was so stunned and overawed by what had happened that I could not really give a coherent explanation. Many times in the still watches of the night the wonder of this miracle has caused the writer to ask himself this question, "Why would the Lord deign to save such a worm from certain death?" Perhaps this book is one of the reasons.

It is with joy and thanksgiving that we thus dedicate this book to the Living God who has said in His Word —"For He shall give His angels charge over thee, to keep thee in all thy ways. They shall bear thee up in their hands, lest thou dash thy foot against a stone" (Psalm 91:11,12).

Foreword

We are living in a day when antichrist cults are busy spreading their soul-destroying teachings over the whole earth. If nobody raises up a standard against an enemy, it becomes easy for him to dominate and take full control. We are admonished to, "Earnestly contend for the faith which was once delivered unto the saints" (Jude 3). Holy Scripture also gives us this command: "Study to show thyself approved unto God, a workman that needeth not to be ashamed, rightly dividing the word of truth" (2 Tim. 2:15). In this busy age it is difficult for the average person to have a ready answer to the tricky questions and arguments that wily cult propagandists have forged to "prove" their position.

The author in his book, *Masters of Deception*, has presented a set of scripture "gauges" to apply to the questions and claims of Jehovah's Witnesses. This procedure enables the reader to measure the degree of error in each point submitted by the Witnesses.

This is a volume that has long been needed. Every Pastor and layman should have this book in their library. I have no hesitation in predicting that it will be the means of keeping many from being ensnared by Watchtower error.

NEIL D. CAMERON, *President*
Christian Workers' Tract League
Vancouver, B.C., Canada

Contents

Introduction

We live in a day of unparalleled deception. Untold thousands of unsuspecting people are deceived each year by false cults. Holy Writ informs us that one of the signs of Christ's Second Coming will be that, "Many false prophets shall rise and shall deceive many" (Matt. 24:11). This prophecy of scripture is having its fulfillment today right before our very eyes.

This book is an exposé of one of the most active and highly organized false cults in our day — the so-called Jehovah's Witnesses. These are the people who strongly insist that they alone are the only true Christians in the world today. It is well to remember that everyone else, regardless of his Church affiliation and beliefs, is considered by JW's to be deceived and under the control of Satan. According to the JW's, all Churches and Pastors (especially Evangelical Christians) are slated for destruction and will go down biting the dust at Armageddon. This in brief is the attitude of the JW's towards those who belong to the historic Christian Church.

The sweeping claims and charges levelled against the Christian Church by JW's will be answered in these pages. In this book truth and error shall grapple. The best arguments that the JW's can muster against the doctrines of Evangelical Christianity will be presented. Their many cunningly devised arguments will be answered. This is a book which will lead the reader, step by step, along the dark labyrinths of twisted, heretical Watchtower thinking. We venture into these dark caverns of heretical thought, not just to curse the darkness, but in search of lost souls who have been deceived and blinded by a false gospel. We carry with us a light that will show them the way out of the dismal regions of spiritual confusion and darkness. The light we hold forth is the glorious gospel of our Lord Jesus Christ. This is what dispels the power of darkness and sets the captive free. What we offer to all those who seek the truth are the immortal words of Him who said: "I am the light of the world; he that followeth Me shall not walk in darkness" (John 8:12).

In this book we shall also deal with the JW's use of so-called "Theocratic War Strategy." This is a coined Watchtower expression which denotes that *lying* is sometimes justified. In plain words "Theocratic War Strategy" simply means that JW's can be deceitful and lie to you in order to protect the Watchtower Society from criticism. (See Chapter Nine entitled "Justified Lying".)

The author does not delight in deliberately hurting the feelings of people. We do not rejoice because the devils are subject unto us (Luke 10:17, 20). We rejoice in the fact that our sins are washed away by the Blood of Christ, and because our names are written down in Heaven. However, we just cannot sit idly by while JW's continue to deceive unwary souls with their damnable lies and doctrines of devils. If we fail to answer their false charges, then our silence could be misconstrued by many to mean that the JW's are right. Further, to remain silent while false prophets deceive people is to disobey the following scriptural command: "Earnestly contend for the faith which was once delivered unto the saints" (Jude 3). We cannot remain silent. We dare not remain silent, for precious souls are in the balance. It is the writer's firm intention to make this book a loud, ringing testimony of truth. We have letters that even the blind will be able to see. Yea, we have words that even the deaf shall be able to hear.

In this book we shall be discussing the conflict between light and darkness. Truth and Error are in a life and death struggle — a raging warfare in which the souls of men are at stake. Thousands, yea, tens of thousands, have been deceived by the false cult of which we speak. With impious daring these scripture manipulators have employed their shifty tactics and wilful perversions in order to deceive the unsuspecting. Their trickeries will be exposed in these pages. In the ensuing chapters you will see error after error slink away in defeat; misshapen heretical teachings which bore their way into the minds of the unwary will have the light of God's truth turned on them. Hellish lies that foul the very atmosphere with their poisonous vapourings will be forced to flee before the mighty rushing wind of the Spirit of Truth. The reader will see Truth time and time again emerge victorious, and Error left writhing in the dust of defeat.

We are not so naive as to believe that this book will bring about a mass exodus from the Watchtower Society. We know from much personal experience that we are dealing with those who "love darkness rather than light." There are, of course, exceptions to this rule even within the ranks of the Witnesses. We trust and pray that there may be some JW's who will be honest enough to admit the truth when it is proven to them from Holy Scripture. Unfortunately this rarely happens. The majority of JW's are so fanatically dedicated and committed to the Watchtower Society that no amount of scriptural evidence will ever convince them they are wrong. In dealing with JW's we have found that most of them are possessed with such a spirit of obstinacy that it seems they would prefer to go to Hell rather than admit they had been deceived.

Over the years the writer has personally dealt with scores of JW's. We have spent many long hours debating with them in homes, on the streets, and at their conventions. Quite frankly, we must confess that in all our efforts with these people there is only one conclusion that can be honestly drawn. *Jehovah's Witnesses do not love the truth.* They are only interested in that which might benefit the cause of the Watchtower Society. The reader at this juncture is probably asking himself this question: "If the JW's have such a stubborn attitude, then why waste time writing this book?" This is a fair question and one that deserves an answer. Our primary reason in putting out this volume is to answer the false charges which the JW deceivers hurl against the Christian Church. Our secondary purpose is to try to convince the JW's of their many errors. In most cases this is well nigh impossible seeing that they are so stubborn and stiff-necked. We are well aware that the JW's will scream they are being persecuted because this book has been written. Apparently it is quite permissible for the JW's to print tons of literature denouncing the beliefs of others. But just let someone attempt to answer some of their lies and immediately they scream persecution! "We are being persecuted!"

Another reason this book has been written is to warn new Christians to beware of modern day religious deceivers. Further, the information found in this work will instruct Christians on how to effectively deal with the JW's when they come in contact with them. What is said here will enable Christians to withstand and blunt the ferocity of the Watchtower onslaught which has swept so many into perdition.

Chapter one

CLEARING THE DECKS

Before we begin our study on the JW's, a few objections which some Evangelicals might raise ought to be answered. There are some Christians who object to anything being written or said about another religion. Sad to say, the number of Pastors and laymen who have accepted this *new trend* are legion. These good men sincerely feel that it is ungracious and unkind to condemn another man's religion. This view, although it may appeal to human sentimentality, is contrary to the word of God and is responsible for creating a fertile field wherein the false cults can flourish UNDISTURBED. False religious deceivers have waxed bold and strong because many of the Pastors in our Churches will not speak out against them.

There are many that could rightly be called cream-puff Christians who tell you, "All we need to do is preach the Gospel, and if it becomes necessary God will defend His own Word." Those who espouse this idea claim to have so much "love" that they don't believe in criticising what the devil is doing today. Certainly the Apostle Paul never held such a limp view because he declared: "I am set for the defence of the gospel" (Phil. 1:17). In his day Paul set himself to defend the truths of the gospel. Should not Christians likewise do the same thing today?

There are those who will quickly tell you that the Bible commands us to—"Judge not" (Matt. 7:1). The context, however, clearly reveals that this command to "Judge not" is addressed to a *hypocrite*. This is indeed evident from the words, "And why beholdest thou the mote that is in thy brother's eye, but considerest not the beam that is in thine own eye?" Our Lord then goes on to say, "Thou *hypocrite*, first cast out the beam out of thine own eye" (Matt. 7:5). Certainly this text does not prohibit honest judgment, but it is a warning against hypocritical judgment. Actually the last part of this scripture commands the pharisaical individual to get right with God. After this has been done, he then is in a position to exercise righteous judgment. "Then (after he is right with God) shalt thou see clearly to cast the mote out of thy brother's eye" (Matt. 7:5).

The Bible tells us that Christ issued this warning: "Beware of false prophets" (Matt. 7:15). But how can we beware, and how can we know who the false prophets are unless we judge? The Saviour has commanded us to—"Judge righteous judgment" (John 7:24). Christ also commended a man with these words: "Thou hast rightly judged" (Luke 7:43). The Apostle Paul declared, "I speak as to wise men; judge ye what I say" (1 Cor. 10:15). Paul further states, "He that is spiritual judgeth all things" (1 Cor. 2:15). In the light of these scriptures we totally reject the false notion that Christians are not to judge. Howbeit, there is only one God-given standard by which we are to judge. It is written: "To the law and to the testimony; if they speak not according to this Word, it is because there is no light in them" (Isa. 8:20). The Bible then is the Book by which everything must be judged.

Some well meaning people have accused us of lacking Christian love because we have denounced the teachings of JW's. One wonders just how consistent those who have joined the namby-pamby camp really are. Would those of the wishy-washy persuasion dare accuse Christ of lacking love when He declared: "Ye serpents, ye generation of vipers, how can ye escape the damnation of Hell?" (Matt. 23:33). Would they also dare accuse John the Baptist of not being God's man when he thundered: "O generation of vipers, who hath warned you to flee from the wrath to come?" (Matt. 3:7). Can they say that Elijah did not have God's Spirit on him when he *taunted and mocked* the false prophets of Baal? (I Kings 18:27). Will they dare to say that St. Paul was not in God's will when he denounced Elymas, the sorcerer, with these scathing words: "O full of all subtilty and all mischief, thou child of the devil, thou enemy of all righteousness, wilt thou not cease to pervert the right ways of the Lord?" (Acts 13:10). Have they never read Martin Luther's stinging accusations against the corrupt Church of his day? What will they say about John

Wesley who declared: "False religious teachers are worse than cut-throats, for they murder the souls of men for whom Christ died."

We who are witnesses for Christ have not been sent forth by our Lord to be public relations men. Neither have we been commissioned to be diplomats. Our message is not one of compromise; we do not water down the gospel of Christ so that it is acceptable to the thinking of contemporary man. We are to be as the prophets of old issuing warnings and ultimatums in the name of the Lord. The Bible plainly tells us, "He that believeth and is baptized shall be saved; but he that believeth not *shall be damned"* (Mark 16:16). If this offends the sensitive ears of the wicked and ungodly . . . THEN SO BE IT! Far better for men to be offended in this life, while there is still hope for salvation, than in the world to come.

We make no apology for taking the position that we do against the JW's, apostasy, sin and unbelief. We stand on the same ground with the Apostles and the Reformers. We stand where the Christian martyrs of all ages have stood — on the sure Word of God which is forever settled in Heaven. This book is not a sugar-coated pill. It is a book which exposes the latter day delusion of the Watchtower gospel.

Chapter two

THE HOLY TRINITY

The very fundamentals of the Christian Faith are denied by the Jehovah's Witnesses. Their chief target of attack has ever been the doctrine of the blessed Holy Trinity. With scornful contempt the JW's level their foul indecencies and indignities against the Triune God. These deceivers do not hesitate to boldly announce that — "Satan is the originator of the trinity doctrine" (Let God Be True, p. 101). The JW's even go so far as to blasphemously denounce the Holy Trinity in these profane words: "Nevertheless, sincere persons who want to know the true God and serve him find it a bit difficult to love and worship a complicated, freakish-looking, three-headed God" (Let God Be True, p. 102).

The JW's brand the Trinity doctrine as being "contrary to reason" and therefore reject it. Their objection here is best answered by the fact that many of the great truths of the Bible such as the Virgin Birth, Resurrection, and the Trinity may *seem* contrary to man's reason; but in reality such truths are above the grasp of man's intellect or reason. A Christian accepts the great truths of the Bible not because he claims to fully understand them, he believes them to be true because they are taught in the Bible. The Trinity, therefore, is not contrary to human reason but rather is above the grasp of man's faltering reason. Even as God's ways are far above our ways so is His divine nature, and any God that could be fully fathomed by our finite minds would not be worthy to be called God.

The term Trinity

Another argument the JW's raise is that the doctrine of the Trinity must be false because the actual term "Trinity" is not found in the Bible. This is a rather flimsy point because the JW's own favourite Watchtower terms such as "Millennium" and Theocracy" (God's rule) are also not found in the Bible. The words Millennium, Theocracy and Trinity are merely theological terms which have been coined to express certain great truths that are found in the Bible.

The Trinity in Scripture

The Trinity is first revealed in the opening book of the Bible: "And God said, Let *us* make man in *our* image, after *our* likeness" (Gen. 1:26). This text informs us that man was created not only by God the Father (the One speaking), but also by the other Divine Persons whom the Father was addressing. The words "let us make man" firmly establish that there was a plurality of Divine Persons who participated in the creation of man. These Divine Persons together made man and are spoken of collectively in Gen. 1:27 AS GOD WHO CREATED MAN. The evidence is thus clear and undeniable — the God of Heaven who created man is therefore a plurality of Divine Persons, a Triune God, or a Trinity.

The JW's will argue that there is no such thing as a plurality of Persons in the Godhead. In a vain attempt to disprove the Trinity they will cry aloud, "The Lord our God is one Lord" (Deut. 6:4). What they fail to realize here is that a "plural oneness" or "composite unity" is taught in Holy Writ. Similarly in Gen. 2:24 we read that a man "shall cleave unto his wife and they shall be *one* flesh." Here is a case of plural oneness. Two distinct separate persons are considered by God here to be *one flesh*. Likewise Gen. 1:26 reveals that there is a plurality of Persons within the Godhead. The Father speaks and says to the Son and the Holy Spirit: "Let *us* make man in *our* image." Each of these Divine Persons then had an active part in the creation of man. Yet in Gen. 1:27 we are told that it was God who created man. This thus shows that the God of Heaven is a Triune God or a Trinity.

The Trinity in Creation

THE FATHER CREATES — "O Lord (Jehovah) thou art our Father; we are the clay, and thou our potter; and we are all the work of thy hand" (Isaiah 64:8).

THE SON CREATES — "All things were made by Him (Christ) and without Him was not anything made that was made" (John 1:3).

THE HOLY SPIRIT CREATES — "By His Spirit He hath garnished the heavens" (Job 26:13).

These scriptures firmly establish that the Father, Son and Holy Spirit were all active in the creation. The JW's teach that the Son did have a part in the creation *but only after the Father had first created Him*. The JW's thus reduce Christ to the lowly position of a mere creature. In fact they do not hesitate to say that Christ in His pre-human existence was none other than Michael the archangel. According to the JW theory, the Father supposedly first created the Son (Michael the archangel) and then through the Son He created everything else.

This JW view is most erroneous because the Bible emphatically affirms that no one less than Jehovah God had any part in the creation of the heavens and the earth. This truth is vividly portrayed in Isaiah 44:24.

"I am the Lord (Jehovah) that maketh all things; that stretcheth forth the heavens alone; that spreadeth abroad the earth by myself."

Notice here that it is Jehovah *alone* who has made all things. This Divine utterance clearly proves that no angel or creature participated in the creation as the JW's maintain. The decree of Holy Writ cannot be broken: "Jehovah *alone* stretched forth the heavens." Notwithstanding this fact, there are other scriptures which declare that the Father, Son and Holy Spirit were all active in the creation. Such evidence forces the honest heart to accept the inescapable conclusion that the true Jehovah of the Bible is a Triune God or a Trinity.

The JW's will try to squirm out of this condemning evidence by stating that the Father simply used the Son as a workman to help Him create the universe. The JW's maintain that this is the same thing as an engineer who declares: "See, I built that bridge; however (continues the JW) the engineer who built the bridge used other workmen to help him construct it."

The only thing wrong with this piece of Watchtower logic is the fact that they have carefully omitted the all-important word "alone." The text under discussion reads: "Jehovah *alone* stretcheth forth the heavens" (Isa. 44:24). Their illustration here falls apart at the seams because no engineer would say, "I *alone* built that bridge and by myself I constructed it." How could any engineer possibly say such a thing when he used other workmen to help him construct the bridge? Bear in mind that Jehovah declares in our text that He *alone* created the heavens and the earth. But please remember that the scriptures also teach that the Son and Holy Spirit created the heavens and the earth. In view of this fact one can only conclude that the Creator is a Triune God or a Trinity.

Further proof for the Trinity is given by Christ when He said: "Go ye therefore, and teach all nations, baptizing them in the name of the Father, and of the Son, and of the Holy Ghost" (Matt. 28:19). Let us read this text using the JW definition of the Son and the Holy Spirit. (Keep in mind that the JW's define Christ as a mere creature and the Holy Spirit as just an active force.) Our text would then read: "Baptizing them in the name of the Father, and of a *Creature, and of an Active Force.*" Such a rendering creates a grating effect and is most blasphemous. Paul in his benediction also refers to the Trinity: "The grace of the Lord Jesus Christ, and the love of God, and the communion of the Holy Ghost, be with you all" (2 Cor. 13:14). The same intolerable discord presents itself if we attempt to interpret this text according to JW teaching: "The grace of a *Creature,* and the love of God, and the communion of an *Active Force,* be with you all." How terribly distorted these scriptures become when we interpret them according to JW theology!

Illustrations

Truths that are above the grasp of human reason can sometimes be explained in a limited way by illustration or analogy. The following illustrations will show that three can be one and one can be three.

(1) All are aware that water is "one," yet it is manifested in three forms — liquid, ice, and vapour.

(2) Time is "one," yet it has a three-fold dimension — past, present and future.

(3) The sun is "one" and yet it has a *three-fold manifestation* — light, heat and fire.

(4) Electricity is "one" but it too has a *three-fold manifestation* — motion, light, and heat.

(5) Science tells us that every beam of light has three rays — the actinic (which is invisible), the luminiferous (which is visible) and the calorific (which gives heat).

(6) The universe is "one" and is composed of three basic elements — space, matter and time. Space is composed of three dimensions — length, breadth and height. Space is therefore THREE IN ONE. Matter itself is produced by the *three-fold manifestation* of energy, motion and phenomena.

(7) The human personality is "one," but it involves the three-fold use of the will, intellect and affections. Man's body has three distinct systems in it — the nervous system, the circulatory system, and the digestive system. Yet these three distinct systems are each propelled by the one life force. The Bible tells us that man is made in the image of God (Gen. 1:27). Consequently man himself is a trinity — spirit, soul and body (1 Thess. 5:23).

The JW's make much of the fact that 1 plus 1 plus 1 equals 3. However there are other unities which are far more complex than this simple mathematical equation. There is, for example, the organic unity of a living creature; there is the aesthetic unity of a work of art and there is the unity of nature. Surely the Creator is infinitely more complex than His creation.

It is sheer arrogance for JW's to say that they reject the Trinity doctrine because they don't understand it. We judge a doctrine to be true or false by the standard of God's unerring Word and not by man's faltering human reason. There are many things in this life which we accept as fact even though we cannot fully explain them. For instance, who can explain how a brown cow can take green grass and turn it into white milk, which then can be churned into yellow butter? Who can explain the marvelous process by which bees make honey? Science has never been able to unravel these mysteries. Yet these things are accepted facts even though we cannot completely explain their existence. Likewise the Trinity exists even though we cannot fully understand the Being of our God. Fallen man cannot fully grasp divine realities. Finite minds reel at the thought of infinity. Using this as a comparison, how much more staggering it is to try to plumb the depths of Him who is the Author of Infinity. John Wesley aptly summed it up when he declared, "Bring me a worm that can comprehend a man, and I will show you a man that can comprehend God." The testimony of scripture is that there is one God eternally existing and manifesting Himself in three Persons.

Chapter three

THE DEITY OF CHRIST

The doctrine of the Deity of Christ is the cornerstone of Christianity. To deny this foundational truth is to take the heart out of Christianity. It is characteristic of all false cults to deny the Deity of Christ and the JW's are certainly no exception to this infamous rule. In fact they have earned for themselves the unsavory reputation of being the most militant of all the Christ-denying cults.

We shall begin our study on the Deity of Christ by first answering the misapplied texts and arguments which the JW's use to support their heretical position. Incidentally, the JW view concerning Christ was first popularized by Arius of Alexandria in the fourth century A.D. Arius taught that Jesus was the first creature, who became a second god, inferior to Jehovah. Suffice it to say, this teaching was condemned by the early Church and branded as rank heresy. It was the infamous Charles Taze Russell, founder of the Watchtower Society, who resurrected this ancient heresy. Russell patched this Christ-belittling heresy up somewhat and then palmed it off to his followers as a long lost truth.

The JW's teach that before He came to earth, Christ was none other than the created archangel Michael. Upon His coming to earth Christ supposedly then became merely a perfect man. In a Watchtower article entitled "Was Jesus A God Man?" (April 15, 1956, p. 239), we read these comments:

> "So for Jesus to provide the ransom, he must be a perfect man, no more and no less. Further if Jesus had been a spirit garbed in flesh, he could not really have died at man's hands . . . But the Bible is clear that Jesus did

provide the ransom and that he was a man, not God
clothed in flesh."

Enough has been said here to show what the JW's teach concerning
Christ. We now present the following scriptures and arguments
employed by JW's to support their heretical position.

Misapplied texts

(1) "These things saith the Amen (Christ), the faithful and true
witness, the beginning of the creation of God" (Rev. 3:14).

(2) "Who (Christ) is the image of the invisible God, the first-born
of every creature" (Col. 1:15).

(3) "The LORD (Jehovah) possessed me (Christ) in the beginning
of his way, before his works of old. I was set up from everlasting,
from the beginning, or ever the earth was. When there were no depths
I was brought forth" (Prov. 8:22-24).

(4) Christ said, "I go unto the Father, for my Father is greater
than I" (John 14:28).

(5) Christ said, "Heaven and earth shall pass away, but my words
shall not pass away. But of that day and hour knoweth no man, no,
not the angels which are in heaven, neither the Son, but the Father"
(Mark 13:31-32).

(6) It is written: "The head of every man is Christ, and the head
of the woman is the man, and the head of Christ is God" (1 Cor.
11:3).

(7) "And when all things shall be subdued unto him, then shall the
Son also himself be subject unto him that put all things under him,
that God may be all in all" (1 Cor. 15:28).

(8) "And Jesus said unto him, Why callest thou me good? none is
good, save one, that is, God" (Luke 18:19).

(9) "If Jesus was God, who ran the universe for three days while He
was in the grave?"

(10) "If Jesus was God, who was He praying to in the garden —
himself?"

The Christian answer

The JW's will argue that Christ is a creature because Rev. 3:14 calls Him "the beginning of the creation of God." The Greek word for "beginning" is ARCHE and can correctly be rendered "origin." The JW's are forced to acknowledge this fact because in their own Bible (The New World Translation, 1950 Edition), they render ARCHE at John 1:1 as "originally" in preference to the term "beginning." Thus by their own admission Rev. 3:14 can be translated to mean that Christ is the ARCHE or "origin" of the creation of God. It thus is clear that the reason Christ is called the "origin" or "beginning" of the creation of God is because *He brought creation forth*. Since Christ is the Creator and Originator of all things (John 1:3, Col. 1:16), He would therefore have to be "the beginning of the creation of God." He who brought creation forth is the BEGINNING or ORIGIN of the creation. How could it be otherwise?

The Evangelical view of Rev. 3:14 is most clear in the Amplified New Testament which states: "These are the words of the Amen (Christ), the trusty and faithful and true Witness, the Origin and Beginning and Author of God's creation." Instead of this text teaching that Christ was created as the JW's affirm, Rev. 3:14 actually proclaims that Christ is UNCREATED and hence God — for only God could be the *Origin and Author and Beginning of creation.*

Numerous other translations also corroborate the Evangelical view of Rev. 3:14. The New English Bible declares that Christ is "the *prime source* of all God's creation." The Knox version reads "the faithful and true witness, the *source* through whom God's creation came." Both Williams' and Goodspeed's translations render Christ as — "The Beginner of God's creation" (Rev. 3:14).

First born of all Creation

"He is the image of the invisible God, the first-born of all creation, because by means of him all (other) things were created in the heavens and upon earth . . . All

(other) things have been created through him and for
him. Also he is before all (other) things and by means of
him all (other) things were made to exist" (Col. 1:15-17,
JW Bible).

The JW translation of Col. 1:15-17 falsifies what the Apostle Paul
actually wrote. The translators of the JW Bible have deliberately
added the word "other" here four times. This term "other" does not
appear in any Greek text. Furthermore the Watchtower Society knows
it. Why was this done? They have tampered with God's Holy Word
here in a vain attempt to put Christ on the same level as "other"
created things. The JW's are so bent on degrading Christ to the
position of a mere creature that they will even add to the Word of God
to accomplish their purpose. No reliable translation would dare tamper
with a doctrinal text in this fashion.

When these facts are revealed to JW's, they will quickly reply that
their four-fold use of the word "other" at Col. 1:16-17 APPEARS EACH
TIME IN BRACKETS. The JW's will argue that since they have put the
word "other" in brackets this shows that their rendering of Col. 1:16-
17 is not a dishonest one. They will tell you this was done merely for
the sake of clarification. Brackets or no brackets, they have deliberately
inserted the word "other" here four times and this changes the meaning
of the whole text completely. Further, they are being hypocritical
about this matter because in their 1950 edition of the New Testament
the JW's DID NOT PUT THEIR FOUR-FOLD USE OF THE WORD "OTHER"
IN BRACKETS! Moreover, the only reason they now have "other" in
brackets in their 1961 Bible is because they have been pressured into
doing it. This pressure has come from Evangelical scholars who
exposed their dishonest rendering of Col. 1:16-17 when it first
appeared.

The JW's claim that Christ is created because Col. 1:15 hails Him
as "the first born of every creature." It is erroneous to conclude that
Christ is the "first created" simply because He is the first born. These
two terms are not synonymous. Greek scholars inform us that the
Greek term for "first created" is PROTOKTISIS whereas the Greek word
for "first born" is PROTOTOKOS. One can see that they are two entirely
different words.

It is significant that in Col. 1:15 the Apostle Paul deliberately avoids using the Greek term for "first created" and instead chooses the Greek word for "first born." Surely this means something! It expressly declares that Paul disagrees with the JW's concerning the Person of Christ. If Paul had wished to express the JW view, THEN WHY DID HE NOT USE THE GREEK WORD FOR "FIRST CREATED"? Since Paul didn't do this, we can only conclude that Christ *is not the first created* as the JW's falsely teach. Moreover, since Christ is not the first created then neither can He be the second created. The real truth of the matter is that Christ is not created, but eternal. This becomes evident when we read the following scripture: "He (Christ) is before all things" (Col. 1:17). Since Christ is before all things, He therefore existed before the start of creation and is thus eternal. Only God could be before all things. As this term is in reference to Christ, He therefore is uncreated and eternal, the One who is from everlasting (Micah 5:2).

If this term "first born" does not mean first created, then what does it mean? In Bible days the Jews understood the term "first born" to refer to Position and Rank. In other words the first born son (according to Jewish custom) was his father's heir. All that his father possessed was his. How fitting then that this term "first born" should be applied to Christ. This term signifies that the Son is the "appointed Heir of all things" (Heb. 1:2). Let us not forget that the context clearly reveals that all things in heaven and earth were created by the Son and for the Son (Col. 1:16-17). And by virtue of this fact the Son stands as Ruler, Creator, and First Born — *the appointed Heir* of all creation.

Wisdom brought forth

"Jehovah possessed me (Wisdom) in the beginning of his way, before his works of old, I was set up from everlasting, from the beginning, or ever the earth was. When there were no depths I was brought forth" (Prov. 8:22-24).

The Son of God is spoken of here as being the personification of wisdom. The JW's insist that this text teaches that Jehovah created Wisdom (interpreted as the Son) in the beginning of his way. The argument which the JW's advance from this text really proves too much. The Son cannot be created, for He is spoken of here and elsewhere as the Wisdom of God. How can the "Wisdom" of God be created? Surely God's wisdom must be as eternal as Himself.

The Apostle Paul makes this stupendous statement: "Christ the power of God and the wisdom of God" (1 Cor. 1:24). Note that Christ is called here the power and wisdom of God. Now if there was a time when Christ did not exist — then there must have been a time when THE POWER AND WISDOM OF GOD DID NOT EXIST! Since the power and wisdom of God are eternal, then Christ must be eternal because He is the Power and Wisdom of God.

What does this text mean? "The LORD possessed me (Wisdom) in the beginning of his way, before his works of old." In the dim ages of antiquity, before the worlds were formed, beyond the beginning of time, it was decreed in the eternal counsels of God that the Son of God would be the wisdom and power by which the worlds were to be made. This is not to say that the Son was created at this point. For Wisdom declares, "I was daily His (the Father's) delight, rejoicing *always* before Him" (Prov. 8:30). The Son was *always* beside the Father. But now Wisdom becomes the Father's Master Workman. It is in this sense that Wisdom "was brought forth"; or to put it another way, the Wisdom of God became active in creation (Col. 1:16).

The Father greater

> Christ said, "I go unto the Father, for my Father is greater than I" (John 14:28).

Christ here is speaking as a man. We must remember that in the Incarnation our Lord voluntarily limited Himself. While upon earth the Saviour's attributes of Deity were held in abeyance; namely, His omniscience, omnipresence and omnipotence. The miracles which Christ performed were done through the power of the Holy Spirit.

Christ performed His mighty works not as God (which He ever remained) but as man. Even though the attributes of Deity were not fully used by Christ during His earthly ministry, He was still God manifest in the flesh (1 Tim. 3:16).

When the Son of God was upon earth, the Father was indeed greater than the Son. However, it is equally as true that when God's Son walked this fallen world, *He was even less than Himself!* This truth is made abundantly clear when we recall that Christ "took upon Him the form of a servant, and was made in the likeness of men. And being found in fashion as a man, HE HUMBLED HIMSELF, and became obedient unto death, even the death of the cross" (Phil. 2:7).

It would be sheer arrogance for a mere creature to say, "THE ETERNAL FATHER IS GREATER THAN I AM." In what way was the Father greater than the Son? And we might also ask, "In what way was the Son of God even *less* than Himself?" Christ here is certainly not comparing His own human nature with the Divine nature of the Father. The context clearly reveals that Christ is speaking words of comfort to His disciples. What Christ is comparing here is His present earthly condition with the celestial glory which would soon be His once again. In other words, Christ is saying here that His glorification and return to the Father would enable Him to bestow greater blessing and greater power unto His disciples. "Greater works than these shall he (the believer) do; because I go unto my Father" (John 14:12). Christ said unto His disciples: "If ye loved me, ye would rejoice, because I said, I go unto the Father; for my Father is greater than I."

It is thus clear that while Christ was on earth as a humble servant, He was "positionally inferior" to His Father and for this reason could say: "My father is greater than I." However, in essence and in glory the Son is equal with the Father. Christ is equal to the Father in essence because He said, "I and my Father are one" (John 10:30). The fact that the Son is uncreated and eternal (Micah 5:2) is further proof that the Son is equal in essence with the Father. The Son is also equal with the Father in glory, for the Son is the "Lord of Glory" (1 Cor. 2:8). Christ in His High Priestly prayer says, "O Father, glorify thou me with thine own self with the glory which I had with thee *before the world was*" (John 17:5). Christ tells us here that He shared the Father's glory even before the world was created. Hence the Son is equal in glory with the Father. It would be sacrilegious for any creature to dare boast of such a claim. Only one who was equal with the Father could share the Father's glory. It is written: "I am Jehovah; that is my name; AND MY GLORY WILL I NOT GIVE TO ANOTHER" (Isaiah 42:8).

Why Christ did not know the day and hour

> "Heaven and earth shall pass away . . . But of that day and that hour knoweth no man, no, not the angels which are in heaven, neither the Son, but the Father" (Mark 13:31-32).

The JW's interpretation of this text is that God is all-knowing, and since Christ declares here that neither He, nor the angels, know the day and hour of the passing away of the heavens and earth — Christ then cannot be God. It is certainly true that "wisdom and power" are the inalienable attributes of Deity. The Bible tells us, "Power belongeth unto God" (Psa. 62:11); "Wisdom and might are His" (Dan. 2:20). However, let us ever remember that in His Incarnation Christ chose voluntarily not to use the knowledge and power of His inherent Deity. Paul reveals this truth to us when he declares that Christ "HUMBLED HIMSELF" (Phil. 2:8). The Apostle's statement here expresses the thought that Christ temporarily laid aside His attributes of Deity when He walked our fallen world.

Christ conquered the world, the flesh, and the devil not as Deity (which He ever remained) but as perfect man. The attributes of Deity, which were ever inherent in Christ, were held in abeyance until His Resurrection. This is evident by the fact that Christ spoke the following words after His Resurrection: "All power is given unto Me in heaven and in earth" (Matt. 28:18). Since Christ now has all power, He most certainly NOW KNOWS the day and hour of the passing away of the heavens and the earth. The problem which the JW's would like to create from this text has a simple answer. The reason Christ did not know (when He was on earth) the day and hour of this great happening was because He chose not to know. We have all heard of the naval captain who sails in war time under sealed orders. The naval captain does not know the contents of the sealed orders until he decides to break the seal. Likewise Christ voluntarily put a limit on the amount of Divine knowledge which He should use during His earthly ministry. One might well say that when Christ was on earth — HE WAS LITERALLY OMNIPOTENCE RESTRAINING HIMSELF. We find this thought confirmed in the following words of scripture: "Will he plead against me with his great power?" (Job 23:6). The Psalmist also declares that God "did not stir up all his wrath" (Psalm 78:38). These scriptures show that God does not put forth all His power and might to accomplish His purposes.

Head of Christ is God

"But I would have you know, that the head of every man is Christ; and the head of the woman is the man; and the head of Christ is God" (1 Cor. 11:3).

The JW's use this text to show that the Son is subject to the Father. We readily agree that the mediatorial Son is indeed subject to the Father. However, the subjection of the Son to the Father does not necessitate a rejection of the Trinity. Quite the contrary, for within the Godhead there exists the Divine principle of subjection and equality. What we mean is that the Son is both subject to the Father and yet equal with the Father. This is not a contradiction. Rather it is an expression of the highest kind of love when two equals voluntarily submit themselves to each other. Not only is the Son subject to the Father, but the Father also submits Himself to the Son. None can argue against the scriptural fact that the Father is committed to fulfill the wishes and desires of the Son (John 16:23). Likewise the Son is also committed to fulfill the will of the Father. Our text at 1 Cor. 11:3 speaks of a husband and wife relationship. This scripture further suggests that a similar unity exists between the Father and Son. Upon examining this text we find that a woman is in subjection to her husband. However, does this mean that because a woman is in subjection to her husband that she is *less* of a human being than her husband? We know that even though the woman is subject to the man, she is still of the same essence and substance as the man. In other words, the woman is equal in substance to the man and is as much of a human being as her husband despite her subjection. The point here is that the woman is only positionally inferior to the man.

While we are on this theme, let us consider the scripture which speaks of Christ being subject for a time to Mary and Joseph. We read where Jesus "went down with them and came to Nazareth *and was subject unto them*" (Luke 2:51). Does this mean that Jesus was *less* than Mary and Joseph? Certainly such could not be the case. It is clear that Jesus was only "positionally inferior" to His earthly parents for a time. This same principle applies in Christ's relationship with the Father. Even though the Son is subject to the Father, He is still of the same essence as the Father. It was Christ Himself who declared, "I and my Father are one" (John 10:30). Since the Son is of the same essence as the Father, the Son is therefore eternal and most certainly cannot be a creature as the JW's falsely teach.

The Bible tells us that Christ Jesus is the "one mediator between God and men" (1 Tim. 2:5). We gather from this text, as well as 1 Cor. 15:24, that the subjection of the Son to the Father is only temporary; it will last only as long as Christ acts as mediator between God and men. When the Son ultimately puts down all rule and all authority and all power, He then delivers up the kingdom to the Father. When this takes place the mediatorial office of Christ comes to an end. The Son then resumes His former position of equality and glory which He shared with the Father before the worlds were made (John 17:5). The problem with the JW's is that they stress the scriptures which speak of the humiliation of Christ, but ignore the texts which speak of His equality with the Father. Thus they get a distorted view of the magnificence of Christ.

The Subjection of Christ

"And when all things shall be subdued unto him, then shall the Son also Himself be subject unto him that put all things under him, that God may be all in all" (1 Cor. 15:28).

The JW's will argue that this text teaches that the Son will ever remain subject unto the Father. Let us explore the text to see what gems of truth are to be found. This scripture tells us there is a time coming when the mediatorial Son delivers up the Kingdom to God the Father. What does this mean? When we speak of the mediatorial Son, we are referring to His whole mediatorial office which extends back into the eternal ages. In Rev. 13:8 Christ is spoken of as "the Lamb slain from the foundation of the world." The Son was also the mediator whom the Father used to create the worlds (Heb. 1:2). During His earthly life, and after it, and on into eternity, the Son continues to act as Mediator between God and men. The whole span of Christ's mediatorial role involves subjection.

However, there is a time coming when Christ's work as Mediator will finally come to an end. This takes place when the mediatorial Son puts down all rule, all authority, and all power. When this happens the mediatorial office of Christ comes to an end. The Son then enters back into that former state of equality which He shared with the Father before the creation of the universe. Throughout the endless ages of eternity, the Triune God Jehovah will permeate the universe with His celestial love and glory. God will then be immediately known by all. What a glorious destiny awaits the redeemed of the Lord.

Only God is good

"And Jesus said unto him, Why callest thou me good?
none is good, save one, that is, God (Luke 18:19).

The JW's think they have conclusive proof here that Christ is not God. They will draw your attention to the fact that Christ declares here that only God is good. They will further point out that since Christ refused the title of "Good Master", how then can Christ be God? On the surface their argument appears to be a good one. However, let us look at this scripture again.

Upon examination we find that a certain ruler is addressing Christ here as "Good Master." Jesus replies by saying, "Why callest thou

Me good? none is good, save one, that is, God." Please note that the emphasis is on the word, "why". Why callest thou Me good? Keep in mind that Jesus knew the very thoughts and intents of the hearts of all men. Obviously Jesus knew that this ruler did not recognize Him as Deity but only as another master or teacher in Israel. This explains why Christ asked him the question, "Why callest thou Me good?" In effect Christ is saying to this certain ruler, If I am not Deity, but just another good master or teacher in Israel — then don't call me good, for only God is good.

In their determined attempt to rob Christ of His Deity, the JW's would thus take away from Christ even the virtue of His goodness. The JW's would have us believe that Christ is saying in Luke 18:19, that He, the Son of God, is not good for only God is good. It is a scriptural fact that Christ is indeed good because the Bible declares that our crucified Saviour is "the Holy One and the Just" (Acts 3:14). We also read concerning Christ: "Thou wilt not leave my soul in hell, neither wilt thou suffer thine *Holy One* to see corruption" (Acts 2:27). In the light of such scriptures, how can the JW's say that Christ is not good?

The term "Holy One" is a title that belongs exclusively to Deity. In Habakkuk 1:12 we read where Jehovah is also called the Holy One. "Art thou not from everlasting, O Jehovah, my God, mine Holy One." Surely this is concrete proof that since Christ is the "Holy One" (Acts 3:14 and Acts 2:27), and since Jehovah is likewise the "Holy One" (Hab. 1:12), then Jehovah is a Triune God — Father, Son and Holy Spirit — the One who only is good.

Was Jesus unconscious in the grave?

This is a rather silly question and one that hardly deserves a reply. The JW's constantly parrot this question in a vain attempt to discredit the doctrine of the Deity of Christ. For if Christ is God, the JW's will say, then this means that during the three days Christ was in the grave, the universe was running by itself! The Witnesses arrive at this startling conclusion via the following process. They reason that since death is unconsciousness, which is false, this must mean that Christ was unconscious during the three days He was in the grave. Moreover, they say this means that the universe was without its Creator for three days.

Christ rebukes the JW's here even as He did the Sadducees of old with these words: "Ye do err, not knowing the scriptures, nor the power of God" (Matt. 22:29). Death is not extinction of being, and this we shall prove in a later chapter. For the present we shall submit the following two scriptural references which show that Christ was conscious while His body lay in the tomb. Christ makes this declaration: "For as Jonah was three days and three nights in the whale's belly, so shall the Son of Man be three days and three nights in the heart of the earth" (Matt. 12:40).

We would ask the JW's this question: Was Jonah conscious in the whale's belly? The following scripture forces them to admit that he was indeed conscious. "Then Jonah prayed unto the Lord his God out of the fish's belly (Jonah 2:1). The fact that Jonah prayed to God out of the whale's belly is conclusive proof that he was most certainly conscious. Now notice what Jesus says in Matt. 12:40: "For AS JONAH WAS three days and three nights in the whale's belly (and we have established that Jonah was conscious in the whale's belly), so shall the Son of Man be (conscious) three days and three nights in the heart of the earth." Jesus tells us here that He would be as Jonah was in the whale's belly. And since Jonah WAS CONSCIOUS, then Jesus ALSO WAS CONSCIOUS while His body lay in the grave.

The Thief on the cross

Another scripture which proves definitely that Christ was conscious between His death and Resurrection reads: "And Jesus said unto him, Verily I say unto thee, Today shalt thou be with Me in Paradise" (Luke 23:43). This promise of hope made by our Lord to the thief shatters the fabricated Watchtower theory of unconsciousness after death. For if the dead are unconscious, how then could the penitent thief and Jesus meet together in Paradise *that same day*?

The daring Watchtower manipulators attempt to escape the crushing evidence of Christ's words here (which so clearly teach consciousness after death) by stating that this text in the Bible is punctuated
wrongly. According to the JW's, the comma should be placed not
before, but rather *after* the word "today." When so done the text
reads as follows: "Truly I tell you today, You will be with me in
Paradise" (Luke 23:43, JW Bible). The Watchtower's bold attempt
to twist Christ's words here is blocked by the simple fact that if our
Saviour said anything on the Cross or elsewhere, He must, of course,
have said it *on the day He uttered it*. Consequently, it would be
needless for Christ to tell the thief that He was speaking to him on the
day of their execution. Certainly if the thief was capable of knowing
anything, he must have known that Christ was speaking to him on
this day without being told it. In a vain attempt to justify themselves
here, the JW's are forced into telling another untruth in order to
cover up their first lie. Their second untruth consists of the fact that
they accuse Christ of speaking needlessly to the penitent thief. They
twist Christ's words here to make them mean that the thief will obtain
Paradise sometime in the future — but not today. The Witnesses
would have us believe that when Christ said "today", He merely
wanted the thief to know that He was talking to him on the day of
their crucifixion, not that he was promising him Paradise on that particular day. Surely the Saviour never spoke needlessly to any man. It
is written of Christ: "Never man spake like this man." Those who
hold the JW view are left with the conclusion that Christ was speaking only superfluously to the penitent thief. Their attempt to distort
the clear meaning of Christ's words here is further refuted by the fact
that this is the only passage where Jesus uses the word "today". In
many passages Jesus has said, "Verily I say unto you," etc., but He
never added the word "today." We conclude that since Jesus used
the word "today" in Luke 23-43, obviously it could only have been
for the sole purpose of conveying to the penitent thief that they would
be together in Paradise that very day.

We further submit that Christ was conscious while His body lay in
the grave because He was aware of the time element. Christ said to
the Jews, "Destroy this temple, AND IN THREE DAYS, I will raise it up
. . . BUT He spake of the temple of His body" (John 2:19-23). The

fact that Christ says here that He would raise Himself from the dead presupposes that our Saviour was conscious while His body lay in the tomb; otherwise how would He have known when the three days had elapsed?

We know that the JW's will attempt to get around this point by stating that the Father raised Christ from the dead, and, therefore, since the Father raised the Son, it would not be necessary for Christ to be conscious to know when the three days had expired. This seems like a good answer to our claim except that Jesus dogmatically asserts in John 2:19 . . . THAT HE WOULD RAISE HIMSELF FROM THE DEAD.

We do not deny that the Father raised Christ from the dead, for it is written: "This Jesus hath God raised up" (Acts 2:32). Nor do we deny that the Holy Spirit raised Christ from the dead: "But if the Spirit of Him who raised up Jesus from the dead dwell in you . . ." (Rom. 8:11). But neither can we deny that Jesus raised Himself from the dead: "Destroy this temple and in three days I will raise it up." Perhaps someone will say, "But this is a contradiction!" Certainly not. For Holy Writ declares, "This Jesus hath God raised up" (Acts 2:32). And as we have seen, the One God who raised Christ from the dead is Father, Son and Holy Spirit. Thus the true God of the Bible is a Triune God or a Trinity.

Did Jesus pray to himself?

The JW's will often ask the following trick question. "If Jesus was God, who was He praying to in the garden — Himself?" The Bible clearly states that Christ prayed to His Father (Luke 22:42). Within the Godhead are three distinct separate personalities who are co-equal, co-existent and co-eternal. These Divine Three constitute the One Eternal God.

The scriptures teach that the term "God" is used to denote the Father, Son and Holy Spirit either collectively or individually. We have already mentioned that the plurality of Divine Persons who participated in the creation of man at Gen. 1:26 are collectively called God in Gen. 1:27. You will recall that Gen. 1:26 declares:

"And God said, let us make man in OUR image after OUR likeness." This text informs us that man was created not only by God the Father (the One speaking), but man was also created by the other Divine Persons mentioned here as being addressed by the Father. The JW argument that the Father was addressing angels in Gen. 1:26 is invalid because nowhere in scripture is man ever said to have been created *in the image of angels.* The fact of the matter is that these Divine Persons in Gen. 1:26 (who together made man) are collectively called God who "created man in His own image" (Gen. 1:27).

The scriptures further teach that the Father, Son and Holy Spirit are also individually called God. In Psalm 89:26 we read that the Father is called God: "Thou art my Father, my God, and the rock of my salvation." In Isaiah 9:6 we learn that Christ is "the mighty God." In John 20:28 we discover that the Apostle Thomas adored Christ as "my Lord and my God." Paul tells us in Romans 9:5 that "Christ came, who is over all, God blessed forever." The Apostle John hails Christ as "the true God and eternal life" (1 John 5:20). These are just a few of the many scriptures which dogmatically state that Christ is indeed God.

The Holy Spirit likewise is called God. In Acts 5:3-4 we read: "But Peter said, Ananias, why hath Satan filled thine heart to lie to the Holy Ghost . . . thou hast not lied unto men, BUT UNTO GOD."

The JW's not only deny the personality of the Holy Spirit, but they also deny the Deity of the Holy Spirit. The above scripture, however, is a stinging rebuke to their unbelief and denial of the Third Person of the Godhead. You will note that the Bible tells us here that man can lie to the Holy Ghost. Bear in mind that the JW's teach that the Holy Spirit is not a Person but merely God's active force. If the JW view concerning the Holy Spirit is correct — HOW THEN CAN ONE LIE TO AN ACTIVE FORCE? Can one lie to electricity? Certainly not. Neither would one be able to lie to the Holy Spirit if He were (as the JW's teach) merely a force; one can lie only to something which has personality. Further, to lie to the Holy Ghost is, as Peter said, *lying to God.* Thus the Holy Spirit is indeed God, the Third Person of the blessed Holy Trinity.

Getting back to the question at hand, we thus see that when Christ was in the garden He prayed as man to the Father. Our Saviour was both God and man. You will recall that in Mark 12: 35-37, Christ declared Himself to be "David's Lord" as well as "David's Son." Christ then is literally the God-man. This majestic Person so associated Himself with the human race that He is "touched with the feeling of our infirmities," and that He "was in all points tempted like as we are, yet without sin" (Heb. 4:15). Thus Christ was both human and divine. The prophet tells us that Christ is not only "the child born" but also "the mighty God" (Isa. 9:6). Here Deity becomes forever wedded to humanity. The mighty God takes unto Himself man's human nature so that He might bring many sons to glory. So fully does the Messiah of heavenly glory become man that He goes to the very depths of human degradation and suffering to bear our load of sin. As our precious Saviour hangs upon a cruel cross enduring the indignities of sinners, a great sobbing cry can be heard coming from His breaking heart — "Father, forgive them, for they know not what they do" (Luke 23:34). The world was murdering its God.

Paul tells us that if the rulers of this world had known the true identity of Christ — "THEY WOULD NOT HAVE CRUCIFIED THE LORD OF GLORY" (1 Cor. 2:8). Those who crucified Christ did not believe that He was God (and neither do the JW's). The Watchtower of April 15, 1956, p. 239 states: "So for Jesus to provide the ransom, he must be a perfect man, no more and no less." The text which we are now dealing with completely shatters the spurious Watchtower claim that Christ was no more than just a perfect man. The Bible tells us plainly here that Christ was much more. Paul dogmatically states that *it was the Lord of Glory whom they crucified*. The attempt by JW deceivers to degrade Christ to the position of a mere creature, in the light of such incontestable scriptural proof, shows what shameless perverters of the Divine Record they are, guilty of blasphemy and treason against the Eternal God.

We have dealt with the ten best so-called "proofs" which the JW's have against the Holy Trinity and the Deity of Christ. In all honesty we must confess that there is nothing in any of their "objections" which disproves the orthodox position. The scriptures which they submit and twist have been shown to enhance the orthodox position. The JW's have been allowed to empty their arsenal of misapplied texts against the great doctrines of the Trinity and the Deity of

Christ, and now it is our turn to take the offensive against those who would dare to try to rip the crown of Deity from the blessed brow of our Lord and Saviour Jesus Christ. In the next two chapters an array of scriptural evidence will be submitted proving beyond all doubt that the Deity of Christ is indeed taught in Holy Scripture. The evidence will be of such a nature that all the insidious cunning of the legions of Hell will not be able to explain it away.

Chapter four

CHRIST IS WORSHIPPED

One of the strongest proofs for the Deity of Christ is the fact that our Saviour was worshipped by both men and angels. To those who sincerely desire to know the truth about the Watchtower Society, we ask you to seriously ponder the following comments. What are we to think of a religion that claims in one breath to be the only true religion in the world today, yet turns about and says that it is wrong and sacrilegious to worship Christ! This is precisely the position of the JW's. The following evidence will conclusively show that JW's do indeed deny worship to Christ.

In the Watchtower of Jan. 1, 1954, p. 30, this question appears in the Questions from Readers section: "Should we worship Jesus?" The Watchtower takes nearly two pages of fine print to answer this all-important question and then gives this conclusion: "Consequently, since the scriptures teach that Jesus Christ is not a trinitarian co-person with God the Father, but is a distinct person, the Son of God, the answer to the above question must be *that no distinct worship is to be rendered to Jesus Christ now glorified in heaven"* (emphasis ours).

The JW's present more of this kind of venomous error in the July 15, 1959 Watchtower, p. 421, which states: "Certainly for one to believe the teachings of Christ he must know and worship the God that Christ worshipped. *Do not erroneously conclude that Christians are to worship Christ;* that is not what he taught. True, he is a god, a mighty one, but he did not worship himself and he did not teach his disciples to worship him" (emphasis ours).

One wonders just what is behind this Watchtower madness which causes men to dare hurl forth in the name of Christianity such blasphemous untruths. The Watchtower Society denies worship to

Christ because they abhor and despise the glorious Bible truth that
Jesus Christ is indeed the Lord God. For it is written in Exodus 34:14
and Matt. 4:10, that it is only God who is to be worshipped.

Scriptures which prove Christ was worshipped

"And behold there came a leper and *worshipped* him,
saying, Lord, if thou wilt, thou canst make me clean"
(Matt. 8:2).

"Behold, there came a certain ruler and *worshipped*
Him . . ." (Matt. 9:18).

"Then came she and *worshipped* Him saying Lord
help me" (Matt. 15:25).

"Then they (the disciples) that were in the ship came
and *worshipped* Him, saying of a truth thou art the Son
of God" (Matt. 14:33).

"And as they went to tell his disciples behold Jesus met
them saying all hail, and they came and held Him by the
feet and *worshipped* Him" (Matt. 28:9).

In clear unmistakable language these scriptures inform us that
Christ did indeed receive worship. The Witnesses will try to save face
here by raising the following objections. They will say that perhaps
the disciples and certain others did worship Christ, but they were
wrong in doing so. If those who worshipped Christ were doing
wrong, then Christ would certainly have rebuked and corrected them.
Not once, however, did our Saviour ever rebuke or correct anyone
for worshipping Him. Surely this proves that Christ accepted their
worship.

Some JW's will even tell you that they do worship Christ — BUT
NOT IN THE SAME WAY OR SENSE AS THEY DO THE FATHER! This rather
artful dodge is blocked by the fact that even their own Watchtower
book of doctrine (Make Sure Of All Things p. 177, 1953 Edition)
CONDEMNS RELATIVE OR SECONDARY WORSHIP. And on page 178
of this same book even bowing before men or angels is forbidden.

The next time you see a JW, ask him this question. Does the

Watchtower teach that it is wrong for man to worship Christ? When you ask this question the JW's know that you are on to them. This issue is a sore spot with the Witnesses, and they will attempt to throw you off the track by giving the following evasive answers: (1) "What do you mean by the term worship?" (2) "We worship the Father through the Son." (3) "We don't worship Jesus above the Father." The reader will note that not one of these replies is an actual answer to our question. The JW's will dig down deep into their bag of Watchtower tricks in order to avoid answering such embarrassing questions directly. Trying to prove something to a JW is like trying to paint a portrait of a chameleon — just when you think you have the subject defined, he changes colour. The JW's have earned for themselves the reputation of being among the nimblest of all cult propagandists.

In order to get around the many scriptures which clearly state that Christ was worshipped, the JW's will say that the word "worship" found in such texts does not really mean worship at all. This attempt to justify their false position by twisting the plain meaning of words proves futile indeed. In the five texts which we have submitted, showing that Christ was worshipped, the Greek word for worship in each instance is "proskuneo." The JW's have translated "proskuneo" as worship twenty-two times in their own Bible to show that God the Father is to be worshipped. Our point is that if "proskuneo" means worship when it is in reference to the Father, then it must also mean worship when it is in regard to Christ. Not so, shouts the JW! They maintain that "proskuneo" means worship only when it is given to the Father; when it is in reference to Christ, they tell us that it merely means reverence or homage.

We are well aware that in classical Greek literature, and also in the Septuagint, that "proskuneo" is sometimes used for humble and prostrate salutation to man. However, such cannot be said for the New Testament. The writers of the New Testament were careful to use this word "worship" only in the highest sense. The term "proskuneo" is found sixty-one times in the New Testament, and the following is a break down of its usage:

Greek scholars inform us that there are twenty-two cases in which proskuneo is used of worship to God the Father; five instances of

Divine worship used intransitively; fifteen cases where it is used of worship to Christ; seventeen instances where idolatrous worship is condemned, AND ONLY TWO DISPUTED CASES WHERE IT MIGHT BE IN REFERENCE TO MAN. We shall now undertake to examine these two cases.

The first case in which worship is said by some to be given to man is found in the parable of the unmerciful servant: "The servant therefore fell down and worshipped (proskuneo) him, saying, Lord have patience with me, and I will pay thee all" (Matt. 18:26). The Lord mentioned here is also the "certain king which would take account of his servants" (Matt. 18:23). As one reads this parable, he is struck by the fact that the Lord, or King, to whom worship is given is pictured as a type of God. Consequently the worship spoken of here is not actually given to man. Significantly, the last part of this parable relates a similar happening between fellow-men, but here the term "besought" is used in place of worship.

The only other instance in the New Testament where worship might be misunderstood as being given to man is in Rev. 3:9. "Behold I will make them of the synagogue of Satan, which say they are Jews, and are not, but do lie, behold, I will make them to come and worship before thy feet, and to know that I have loved thee."

There are two distinct groups mentioned here. One is called "the synagogue of Satan," and the other group is obviously the glorified Church of Jesus Christ. The Bible teaches that there is a day coming when all wrongs will be made right. Jesus declared, "But I say unto you, that every idle word that men shall speak, they shall give account thereof in the day of judgment" (Matt. 12:36). This speaks volumes! Those in the "synagogue of Satan" belong to the devil; they have hounded and persecuted the true people of God all down through the ages. They make the claim here that they are Jews (God's people), but God says they are liars and impostors.

In the great judgment day those who make up the "synagogue of Satan" will be forced to admit, before the tribunal of heaven, that those whom they hated, despised and maligned actually belonged to God. This phrase, "I will make them to come and worship before thy feet, and to know that I have loved thee," shows that these wicked ones will be brought before the feet of God's redeemed glorified

Church and there made to worship. This is not to say they will be made to worship the glorified Church. Only God is to be worshipped. The worship that the "synagogue of Satan" will be forced to give (before the feet of the glorified Church) will take the form of a confession. Paul tells us just what this confession will be: "That at the name of Jesus every knee should bow, of things in heaven (angels), and things in earth (men), and things under the earth (demons); and that every tongue should confess that Jesus Christ is Lord, to the glory of God the Father" (Phil. 2:10-11).

We thus see that every creature in heaven, earth and hell will be made to worship Christ as Lord whether he wants to or not. This, then, is the worship which the "synagogue of Satan" will be forced to give before the feet of the glorified Church. They will be made to acknowledge the fact that Christ is indeed Lord.

It is thus clear that in the New Testament "proskuneo" only means worship in the highest sense. The claim of the JW.'s that there are instances in the New Testament where proskuneo merely means "reverent salutation" to man has been refuted; hence when the New Testament declares fifteen times that Christ was worshipped, no amount of semantic juggling on the part of JW's can ever alter the fact that Christ was worshipped, and is to be worshipped, and ever shall be worshipped.

Angels worship Christ

"But when he again brings his Firstborn (Christ) into the inhabited earth, he says, and let all God's angels worship him" (Heb. 1:6, JW Bible).

This text delivers a crushing blow to the JW heresy that Christ is not to be worshipped. For here we have undeniable proof right from the Watchtower's own version of the Bible *that angels worship Christ.*

It is strikingly apparent that this text creates some rather thorny problems for the JW's. First, if it is wrong to worship Christ as the Watchtower teaches, then all the holy angels are guilty here of committing a sacrilegious act by worshipping Christ! Secondly, if

Christ is a creature (as the JW's maintain) then the angels in heaven are guilty here of the sinful act of creature worship! Thirdly, Christ cannot possibly be Michael the archangel as the JW's teach, for then Heb. 1:6 would be telling us that the angels in heaven *are worshipping another angel!* But whom do the angels worship? The Bible tells us in Nehemiah 9:6 that the angelic hosts of heaven worship Jehovah. The fact that Christ is worshipped by the angels is positive proof that He is God. Holy Writ verifies this truth for us in Matt. 4:10 —"Thou shalt worship the Lord thy God, and Him only shalt thou serve."

The Watchtower's answer to the question of angels worshipping Christ is most interesting. In the *Questions from Readers* column of the Watchtower dated May 15, 1954, they officially give this answer: "Are you an angel of God in Heaven? If you are, then Hebrews 1:6 applies to you. If you are not one of God's angels in heaven, then Heb. 1:6 is not directed to you — ." It is obvious that the Society is trying to be evasive regarding this matter. Nevertheless, there is one point the Society is forced to reluctantly concede here, and that is, *angels do worship Christ.* Yet at the same time the Watchtower warns its readers that this is of no consequence to them, seeing that they are not angels. It seems from the Watchtower point of view that it is permissible for angels to worship Christ, but if man dares to worship Christ he commits a sinful, sacrilegious act. At this point one is reminded of the following adage: "Oh consistency, thou art indeed a rare jewel."

Father and Son receive the same worship

> "The four and twenty elders fall down before him that sat on the throne, and worship him that liveth for ever and ever, and cast their crowns before the throne saying, (Please note what they say): "Thou are worthy, O Lord (Jehovah) to receive *glory and honour and power;* for thou hast created all things" (Rev. 4:10-11).

This text states that the four and twenty elders worship Jehovah the Father by giving Him "glory and honour and power." It is therefore established that "glory and honour and power" are declared here in scripture to be worship. Keeping this thought in mind let us now read Rev. 5:11-12: "And I beheld, and I heard the voice of many angels about the throne and the beasts and elders: and the number of them was ten thousand times ten thousand and thousands of thousands; saying with a loud voice, worthy is the Lamb (Christ) that was slain to receive *power,* and riches, and wisdom, and strength, and *honour,* and *glory,* and blessing."

Here we behold the magnificent sight of the angelic hosts of heaven rendering unto Christ the highest praise and deepest worship that Heaven can give. You will note that among the angelic expressions of worship given here to the Lamb Christ Jesus are "glory and honour and power." These are the same expressions of adoration and praise that were given to the Father in Rev. 4:10-11, and the Bible plainly states there that it is worship. Now let's be reasonable. If such is worship when it is rendered to the Father (and the JW's admit it is), THEN GLORY AND HONOUR AND POWER IS ALSO WORSHIP WHEN IT IS GIVEN TO CHRIST. Thus we have conclusive proof that Christ is indeed to be worshipped, contrary to the false teachings of the JW's.

Consider also our next text which adds still another link to the unbreakable chain of evidence that Christ is to be worshipped:

"And every creature which is in heaven, and on the earth, and under the earth, and such as are in the sea, and all that are in them heard I saying, Blessing, and honour and glory and power be unto him (the Father) that sitteth upon the throne, and unto the Lamb (Christ) for ever and ever" (Rev. 5:13).

This text describes the awesome sight of every creature in heaven and earth giving unto both the Eternal Father and the Lamb the very highest form of praise, adoration and blessing. No JW can dare say that this homage is not worship. For when this homage is offered unto the Eternal Father, then it cannot be anything else but the very highest form of worship. Further, you will note that the same expressions of adoration and praise are repeated here that were given to the Father alone in Rev. 4:11. And in Rev. 4:10 such expressions of praise are plainly called worship. This text thus proves conclusively

that Christ is to be worshipped by both heaven and earth, because the
same homage and worship that is given to the Father here is also
rendered to the Lamb Christ Jesus. If Christ is not God as the Witnesses maintain, then this text teaches us that A MERE CREATURE
RECEIVES THE SAME ADORATION AND HOMAGE AND WORSHIP AS DOES
THE ETERNAL FATHER HIMSELF!

Prayer is worship

In the Old Testament the Hebrews worshipped Jehovah *by calling
upon His name in prayer.* Likewise in the New Testament, Christians
worshipped their Risen Lord by calling upon the name of Jesus in
prayer. In Thayer's Greek - English Lexicon (page 239) the
expression "to call upon the name of the Lord" is translated "to
invoke, adore, worship the Lord, i.e., Christ."

Surely prayer is to be made only to God. Each prayer to Christ
in the New Testament is therefore an act of true worship. You will
recall that in Acts 7:59, Stephen prayed directly to Christ and said,
"Lord Jesus, receive my spirit." Remember that the phrase "to call
upon the name of the Lord" means to invoke, adore and worship.
This is precisely what Stephen was doing here with his last dying
breath. HE WAS INVOKING AND ADORING AND WORSHIPPING JESUS.
If Christ is not God, then Stephen is guilty of praying to a creature!

Another parallel passage dealing with this same topic reads: "To
them that are sanctified in Christ Jesus, called to be saints, with all
that in every place *call upon the name of Jesus Christ our Lord,*
both theirs and ours" (1 Cor. 1:2).

Just think of the tremendous import of these words. *All saints in
every place* are calling upon the name of Christ our Lord. This means
they are invoking and adoring and worshipping Jesus. They are
bringing to His attention great pressing needs that God alone can
meet. The deepest longings and aspirations of the human heart are
being expressed to Christ in prayer. The 'Altogether Lovely One'
gathers up into His nail-scarred hands the woven tissue of our prayers.
He hears the faintest cry of the weakest soul. The one who is lost in

sin and shame cries unto Jesus for forgiveness and is abundantly pardoned and cleansed. Nothing escapes His gaze. He hears all and comprehends all. Yea, His ear is ever open unto the cry of every burdened soul. With sighs of anguish and sobs of grief men pour their hearts out to Jesus in prayer. Tears that are shed to Jesus in prayer become a majesty of utterance. Surely this is the very essence of worship. Did not Jesus say, "Come unto Me, all ye that labour and are heavy laden, and I will give you rest" (Matt. 11:28)? How else do we come to Christ but by calling upon His name in prayer? When the Hebrews in the Old Testament called upon the name of Jehovah, it meant they were worshipping Jehovah. Similarly, when Christians in the New Testament called upon the name of Christ it was an act of worship to Christ. How could it be otherwise? When a Satanist calls upon the name of the devil, we say he is worshipping the devil. When people in Asia call upon the name of Buddha, we say, and rightly so, that they worship Buddha. Likewise when Christians call upon the name of Christ in prayer, they are worshipping Christ.

The evidence that Christ was worshipped in the Bible is indeed massive and conclusive. The twisted blind pride of JW's will not allow them to accept the irrefutable evidence which has been submitted proving that Christ is to be worshipped. As one JW so aptly expressed it: "If the Society is wrong, then we will go down with the Society."

Chapter five

THE WORD — WHO IS HE?

Christians all down through the ages have used the text of John 1:1 to prove that Christ is God. This text reads: "In the beginning was the Word (Christ), and the Word was with God, *and the Word was God.*" When confronted with this text which so clearly shows that Christ is indeed God, the Witnesses will simply say that they do not accept this scripture as it reads in the King James Bible *because it is translated wrongly!* In reply to their claim here we ask the following question. What about the Revised Version, the American Standard, Young's, the Douay and other versions of the Bible which read the same as the King James at John 1:1? Are these also mistranslated? The JW's will reply with a hissing "YES" to this question.

The Witnesses will try to escape the condemning evidence of John 1:1 by boldly mistranslating this text in their New World Translation Bible to read: "Originally the Word was, and the Word was with God, and the Word was a God." Their attempt to reduce Christ to the position of "a god" — a secondary god, is refuted by the following evidence. In the Watchtower of March 1st., 1959, page 150, the JW's stoutly maintain that "the one and only true God is Jehovah." This is indeed correct. However, since Jehovah is the one and only true God (and the Witnesses have just admitted this), then logically EVERY OTHER GOD EXCEPT JEHOVAH MUST BE A FALSE GOD. We thus see that the Witnesses unwittingly make Christ out to be *a false god* in John 1:1 by declaring that He is "a god," but not the God Jehovah. The Witnesses admit that it is impossible for TWO true Gods to exist. They have admitted this by the very fact that the Watchtower has stated, "the one and only true God is Jehovah."

Their "a god" theory is further refuted by the fact that Jehovah makes this declaration: "See now that I, even I am He, *and there is no God with me*" (Deut. 32:39). What does Jehovah say here? He declares, "There is no God with Me." Where, then, did the Watchtower Society ever dig up the teaching that their big God Jehovah has a smaller god called Christ with Him in Heaven? According to this text there is only one God in Heaven and that one God is Jehovah. There is no such thing as any created lesser god in Heaven as the Witnesses teach. Those of the Watchtower persuasion are forced here to accept either one of two things. Either they must believe (as all true Christians do) that Christ is one with the Father, and is also Jehovah, or else they must believe that Christ is not even "a god." There is no other alternative. The Witnesses are here caught in their own heretical trap.

The announcement made by Jehovah in Isaiah 43:10 also exposes their "a god" fallacy: "Before Me there was no god formed, neither shall there be after me." If there was no god formed *before* or *after* Jehovah, then the JW's are certainly teaching heresy when they proclaim that Jehovah the big God created Jesus the lesser god.

The logic behind the Evangelical position concerning John 1:1 is unanswerable. By falsely rendering Christ as "a god" in John 1:1, the JW's thus place themselves in a dilemma from which they can never logically escape. The Witnesses here have been weighed in the balance of logic, reason and Holy Scripture and are found wanting. The JW's will often quote Isaiah 1:18 to the unsuspecting householder: "Come now and let us reason together." Well, we have certainly done that here and what have we discovered? We have seen that the JW's believe in two gods; yet the Bible teaches there is only one true God. We have also learned that they believe their big God Jehovah has supposedly created a smaller god called the Logos or Christ. It doesn't seem to bother JW's that such a view is utterly contrary to the truth revealed at Isaiah 43:10. You will recall that in this text Jehovah emphatically affirms there was no god created either before or after Him. Christ then cannot be "a god," a secondary god, as the Witnesses make Him out to be in John 1:1. Thus the orthodox rendering of John 1:1 is indeed correct, and no trick of exegesis can ever do away with the fact that — "the Word was with God and the Word was God."

The mighty God

> "For unto us a child is born, unto us a son is given: and the government shall be upon His shoulder: and His name shall be called Wonderful, Counsellor, The mighty God, The Everlasting Father, The Prince of Peace" (Isaiah 9:6).

The prophet Isaiah hails Christ here as "The Mighty God." The JW's will attempt to slide around this verse by saying that Christ is "a mighty god," but not the Almighty God. Realizing that this text contradicts their erroneous position, the JW's attempt to squash Isaiah's testimony that Christ is God by bringing into play their theory of two gods. It has been previously shown that Christ cannot possibly be a secondary god because there is only one true God (Isa. 43:10).

Those who adhere to the JW position are forced to conclude that there must be two mighty Gods in Heaven. This becomes evident when you consider that not only is Christ called "the mighty God," but Jehovah likewise is termed the mighty God in Isaiah 10:21 — "The remnant shall return, even the remnant of Jacob, unto the mighty God." (We know from Exodus 3:6 that Jehovah is the God of Jacob.) Jehovah is also called the Mighty God in Psalm 50:1 and Jer. 32:17-18. Thus the Bible clearly teaches that Jehovah likewise is the mighty God. Therefore Christ, who is one with the Father, is also Jehovah because He too is called the mighty God in Isaiah 9:6. The testimony of scripture is clear — there is only one God. Jehovah affirms this truth in these words: "I am the first, and I am the last, and besides Me there is no God. "Is there a God besides Me? yea, *there is no God;* I know not any" (Isaiah 44:6, 8).

Will Christ perish?

> "Thus shall ye say unto them, the gods that have not made the heavens and the earth, even they shall perish

from the earth, and from under these heavens" (Jer. 10:11).

The JW's teach that Christ is not the Creator. This is verified by the fact that the following statement appears as a sub-heading in one of their books: "Jehovah the Only Creator."[1] Please remember that when the JW's speak of Jehovah, they mean only the Father. In regard to Christ they brand Him (in His pre-human existence) as a created lesser god, other than and inferior to Jehovah the Creator.

Those who accept the Watchtower teaching regarding Christ will be shocked to learn the following. According to Jer. 10:11, all gods that have not made the heavens and the earth shall perish. What does this mean? It clearly means that if the JW's are right and Christ is not the Creator, but is merely some sort of secondary "a god," *then Christ will perish!* What ! ! ! Whether JW's like it or not, logic demands that this would have to be the case because Jer. 10:11 dogmatically states: "The gods that have not made the heavens and the earth, *even they shall perish."* This is the sort of heretical conclusion one comes to when he accepts the error laden teachings of the Watchtower Society.

My Lord and my God

The following text is a most difficult one for JW's to explain away: "And Thomas answered and said unto Him (Jesus), My Lord and my God" (John 20:28). In clear unmistakable language the Apostle Thomas adores the Risen Christ here as his Lord and God. We must remember that the Apostle Thomas was a Jew brought up under the law of Moses. The Jews believed in and worshipped but one God, even Jehovah. If Christ is not truly the Lord God then Thomas is guilty of idolatry here. And what is still worse, Christ would be guilty of accepting unrightful homage! But the context bears out that Christ accepts Thomas' declaration of faith. Jesus says here to this once doubting apostle, "Because thou hast seen Me, thou hast believed, blessed are they that have not seen, and yet have believed" (John

---

[1] See "Make Sure Of All Things," p. 79, (1953 Edition).

20:29). Thus the Bible does indeed teach that Christ is the Lord God, even as the historic Christian Church has ever taught.

The JW's will attempt to squirm out from under this crushing weight of scriptural evidence in the following slippery fashion. They will tell you that Thomas does not really call Jesus his Lord and God here. After all, they will say, Thomas was so awe-struck by the appearance of the resurrected Christ that he burst forth with the *exclamation,* "My Lord and my God! ! !" The smiling JW will then sit back and say to the inquiring householder: "Now, doesn't that make sense!" In other words we are supposed to believe that Thomas got so excited here that he forgot himself AND TOOK THE LORD'S NAME IN VAIN! This piece of face-saving trickery is exposed by the clear words of our text: "And Thomas answered and said UNTO HIM (that is, he said it to Jesus), My Lord and my God" (John 20:28). It is an undeniable fact that Thomas here is addressing his statement to Jesus. Therefore Thomas' statement is not an exclamation. The words of Thomas were clearly given to Jesus and are a statement of fact. All the shifty tactics of JW's can never alter the scriptural declaration that Christ is clearly called Lord and God in John 20:28.

The JW's have still another trick of words which they will use to try and break Thomas' testimony that Christ is indeed the Lord God. In their booklet "The Word: Who Is He? According to John" p. 51, they make this statement: "So if Thomas addressed Jesus as 'my God,' Thomas had to recognize Jesus' Father as the God of a God, hence as a God higher than Jesus Christ, a God whom Jesus himself worshipped."

If Christ is "a god" different from Jehovah, then we could say there is "the God of a god." However, we have already shown from the Bible that it is utterly impossible for two true Gods to exist (Deut. 32:39, Isaiah 43:10). The whole tenor of scripture rings forth the refrain that there is only one true God eternally existing in the Persons of the Father, Son, and Holy Spirit. All the verbal juggling of Watchtower inspired trick artists can never alter the express declaration of John 20:28. "And Thomas answered and said unto Him (that is, he said it to Jesus), *my Lord and my God.*"

The true God

> "We are in Him that is true, even in His Son Jesus
> Christ. THIS IS THE TRUE GOD and eternal life" (I John
> 5:20).

This scripture plainly tells us that Christ is "the true God and
eternal life." The JW's will argue that this is not correct. They have
translated this verse in their Bible to read, "And we are in union with
the true one, by means of his son Jesus Christ. This is the true God and
life everlasting." The JW's will tell you that the "true one" spoken
of here is God the Father, and that it is He (God the Father) whom
John is actually calling "the true God and eternal life." It seems that
every scripture which contradicts Watchtower teaching has to be
twisted out of shape and robbed of its real meaning. However, the
Bible is its own best interpreter. You will note that the One whom
John hails here as "the true God" is also called the "eternal life."
In other words He who is the "eternal life" is the true God. Surely
there can be no doubt that Christ is the "eternal life." This is proven
by the fact that John declares, "That *eternal life* which was with the
Father, and was manifested unto us" (1 John 1:2). It is clear from
this text that Christ is the eternal life. We thus have positive scriptural
proof that John is most certainly referring to Jesus when he announces: "We are in Him that is true, even in His Son Jesus Christ, THIS
IS THE TRUE GOD AND ETERNAL LIFE."

It is glaringly evident that JW's will resort to any kind of trickery
and subterfuge in order to get around scriptures which contradict their
false teachings. One can only say that the devotees of this cult
certainly deserve the championship belt for their exegetical juggling
of the scriptures.

Father calls the Son, God

> "But unto the Son He saith, Thy throne, O God, is for
> ever and ever" (Heb. 1:8).

The JW's are constantly labouring to prove that Christ is not God. This passage of scripture is a sound rebuke to their denial of the Deity of Christ. Here the Eternal Father sets forth in most explicit language the Deity of Christ. In this scripture the Father ascribes to the Son the full deific title of God. Not only does the Father here call the Son "God", but He announces that the Son's throne "is for ever and ever." Surely this could not be said of any creature. The Father and Son are one (John 10:30), and by virtue of this fact they share the throne of Heaven. Holy Writ makes this fact crystal clear in these words: "And there shall be no more curse; but the *throne of God and of the Lamb* shall be in it, and His servants shall serve Him" (Rev. 22:3).

We thus see that the throne of Divine glory, from whence flow the streams of celestial joy and love, is called "the throne of God and of the Lamb." Hence Christ is most certainly co-equal with the Father, even as the Christian Church has ever taught, because the Father and Son both occupy the throne of Heaven. Let this statement have its full weight. The possessor of the heavenly throne of glory is the eternal God. Since Christ shares the Father's glory (John 17:5), and since He has said, "All things that the Father hath are mine" (John 16:15), and because the heavenly throne of glory is called "the throne of God and of the Lamb," Christ then is indeed God even as the Father has so stated in Heb. 1:8.

Father and Son are one

How did the Jews understand Christ's claim when He declared, "I and my Father are one" (John 10:30). Was Christ merely saying here that He was one in "agreement, purpose and organization" as the JW's teach? NO! The context clearly bears out that Christ was claiming unity of essence with Jehovah.

If Christ was simply saying to the Jews here in John 10:30 that He was one in agreement and purpose with Jehovah, THEN HE WOULD BE SAYING NO MORE THAN WHAT THE PROPHETS HAD SAID BEFORE HIM! But the fact remains that Christ was saying much more than this because in the very next verse, "the Jews took up stones again to stone Him" (John 10:31). And in verse 33 we are told the reason they wanted to stone Christ: "For a good work we stone thee not; but for blasphemy, and because that thou being a man *makest thyself God.*" It is very clear then that when Christ said, "I and my Father are one" — He was claiming absolute equality with Jehovah the Father.

The JW's will argue that Christ is one with the Father only in the same sense as believers are one with the Father and Son. Listen to what they have to say: "The plain truth reveals itself, that is, just as Christ and his body members are regarded as one, so are Jehovah and Christ regarded as one. They are all one in agreement, purpose and organization."[1] The JW's attempt to back up their claim here by quoting John 17:20-22. "Neither pray I for these alone, but for them also which shall believe on me through their word; that they all may be one; as thou, Father, art in me, and I in thee, that they may also be one in us; that the world may believe that thou hast sent me. And the glory which thou gavest me I have given them, that they may be one, even as we are one."

The JW's conclude from this text that the oneness which Christ shares with the Father is the identical same oneness which believers have with Christ. This idea is certainly false as the following will show. If each Christian is one with Christ as Christ is one with the Father, then each Christian should be able to say, "I (John Doe) and the Father are one." He would also be able to claim, "For what things soever He (the Father) doeth, these also doeth (John Doe) likewise" (John 5:19). Again, "All men should honour (John Doe) even as they honour the Father" (John 5:23). And again, "All things that the Father hath are mine" (belong to John Doe). We could go on and on to show how ridiculous it is to believe (as the JW's do), that there is the same oneness between Christ and believers as exists between Christ and the Father. The context of John 10:30 clearly reveals that there is A UNIQUE ONENESS BETWEEN THE FATHER AND SON, which no creature can ever share. When Jesus said, "I and my Father are one," He was claiming equality with the Eternal God. And as we have pointed out, the Jews understood Him to mean

---

[1] "Let God Be True" p. 104.

nothing less than this because they attempted to stone Him for blasphemy. The attempt of JW's to wilfully pervert the clear meaning of John 10:30 has been refuted. Let us never forget that the JW's deny the Deity of Christ, even as did those who crucified Him.

Only God knows the thoughts of men

> "Then hear thou in heaven thy dwelling place, and forgive, and do, and give to every man according to his ways, whose heart thou knowest, for thou (Jehovah) *even thou only* knowest the hearts of all the children of men" (1 Kings 8:39).

Holy Scripture informs us here that it is Jehovah *alone* who knows the hearts of all the children of men. No angel or creature or demon has the power to probe the inner sanctum of men's hearts. This is a right reserved for God alone. Yet we read concerning Christ that He certainly knew the thoughts and intents of the hearts of all men. Hear what the scripture saith: "But when He (Jesus) perceived their thoughts, He answering said unto them, What reason ye in your hearts?" (Luke 5:22). Also in John 2:24 we read: "That Jesus did not commit Himself unto them, because He knew all men, and needed not that any should testify of man: *for he knew what was in man.*" Again, "And Jesus *knowing their thoughts* said, wherefore think ye evil in your hearts?" (Matt. 9:4).

Since Jesus knew the very thoughts and intents of the hearts of all men, then no juggling of the text can offset the fact that Jesus is none other than Jehovah manifest in the flesh (1 Tim. 3:16). Remember, it is Jehovah alone who knows the hearts of all the children of men (1 Kings 8:39). The JW's will try to dodge the truth of this text by saying that Jehovah granted Christ special power to know the thoughts of men. We know most assuredly that Jesus could not possibly know the thoughts of all men unless He was God. The scripture cannot be broken: "For thou (Jehovah) even thou only knowest the hearts of all the children of men." It is well for JW's to remember that it is impossible for God to lie (Heb. 6:18), and that Jehovah has declared in Psalm 89:34 — "My covenant will

I not break, nor alter the thing that has gone out of my lips." The fact that Christ knew the hearts of all men is clear proof that He is the Lord God of Heaven (1 Cor. 15:47).

Lord of lords

> "These shall make war with the Lamb, and the Lamb shall overcome them; for He is Lord of lords and King of kings . . ." (Rev. 17:14).

The Lamb Christ Jesus is hailed here as "Lord of lords." What does this expression actually mean? It can only mean that He who is the "Lord of lords" is above every other lord in the universe. The JW's are confronted here with a sticky problem which is well nigh impossible for them to answer. Remember, the JW's believe that the Lord Jesus Christ is different from and inferior to the Lord Jehovah. In other words the JW's believe in two Lords. They believe that Jehovah is the big Lord and Jesus is a lesser Lord. Yet at Rev. 17:14 it is Christ who is called "Lord of lords." Does this therefore mean that Christ is now a greater and higher Lord than even the Lord Jehovah? We know that such a question is ridiculous. However, if the JW view is correct, namely that Christ is a secondary Lord different from Jehovah, then this title "Lord of lords" would logically make Christ higher than all other Lords in the universe, including Jehovah! This by itself sufficiently shows just how absurd is the JW position.

The Trinitarian concept of God does not produce the problems which the JW's will have to grapple with here. True Christians have always believed that the Father and Son are one (John 10:30). And by virtue of this fact the Father and Son share the same titles. The Father is God (Psa. 89:26). The Son is God (Heb. 1:8). The Father is Saviour (Isa. 43:10). Likewise the Son is Saviour (Luke 2:11). Scripture declares that the Father is our Creator (Isa. 64:8), but so is the Son our Creator (Col. 1:16). Getting back to the scripture at hand, we find that not only is the Son "Lord of lords," but Jehovah of the Old Testament is likewise called "Lord of lords" (Deut. 10:17). Surely there cannot be *two Lord of lords!* Yet this is precisely what the JW's are logically forced to believe. For if Christ is not Jehovah, but an inferior secondary Lord, then there are indeed two Lord of lords! I suppose the JW's will try to tell us now that the greater "Lord of lords" is in the Old Testament, whereas the lesser "Lord of lords" is in the New Testament. Their false teaching that Christ is a creature is heretical nonsense.

First and last

> "Thus saith the Lord (Jehovah) the King of Israel, and his redeemer the Lord (Jehovah) of hosts; *I am the first and I am the last,* and beside me there is no God" (Isa. 44:6).

Jehovah declares most emphatically here that He is "the first and the last," and the only God. Howbeit at Rev. 1:17 it was Christ who announced, "Fear not, I AM THE FIRST AND THE LAST, and, behold, I am alive for evermore, Amen, and have the keys of hell and of death." If Christ is not God then there are *two firsts and two lasts!* This is the absurd conclusion one is logically forced to accept as a JW.

In their booklet "The Word Who Is He?" (page 45), the Society attempts to get around this embarrassing scriptural evidence by suggesting that Christ was merely "the first and last in the matter of resurrection . . . He was the first one on earth that God raised from the dead to be 'alive for evermore.' He is also the last one whom God raises thus directly." This is an arbitrary interpretation obviously designed to keep Rev. 1:17 from saying that Christ is God. It doesn't matter how they cut this scripture up, they can refine it, spiritualize it, twist it, and explain it away; the fact still remains THEY BELIEVE IN TWO FIRSTS AND TWO LASTS! If we think the matter out, they have a number one "first and last" who is God. Then they also have a number two "first and last," who was not always the first and last, but who became *a second* "first and last" when He was thirty three years old! What utter nonsense! Christ is called the "first and last" because He is the Eternal One. As far back into eternity as you want to go, Christ was there. Understandably, Christ is the "first" because there was no one before Him. Christ is also called the "last" because in the endless ages to come He will always be there. Yea, He is the self existent "I AM" of John 8:58; subsequently "of His kingdom there shall be no end" (Luke 1:33).

The ascension of Christ

One of the great truths of the Bible is the doctrine of the Ascension of Christ. There are scriptures connected with this great theme which positively assert that Christ is God. The JW's tell us, "Jesus was raised from the dead a spirit creature" (Make Sure Of All Things p. 429). Such a view is utterly contrary to scripture as the following will show. In Psalm 47:5 we have this prophecy concerning the ascension of Christ: "God is gone up with a shout, the LORD (Jehovah) with the sound of a trumpet." Certainly this text is speaking to us concerning the ascension of Christ. For it was the Son of God who died for our sins, and who rose from the dead the third day, and who ascended on high. Please note that the One who has "gone up" is called the Lord God Jehovah. Here we have it! This is positive scriptural proof that Christ is indeed the Lord God and not a spirit creature as the JW's falsely teach.

What rejoicing there must have been when Christ ascended into Heaven. Our text tells us that God shouted when He went back into Heaven. Oh, what a shout that must have been. It was a shout of joy! It was a shout of triumph! It was a shout of victory! Our God was happy. The Saviour had just fought the battle of the ages. He had destroyed the power of the devil (Heb. 2:14). Jesus had spoiled evil principalities and powers and made an open show of them (Col. 2:15). Hallelujah! What a Saviour! He met man's greatest enemy — death — face to face and defeated him.

The Bible declares that when Christ died He went down into Hell (Acts 2:27). From Christ's account of the rich man and Lazarus (Luke 16: 19-23), we learn that Hades was divided into two sections. Each section separated from the other by a great gulf (Luke 16:26). One part of Hades was a place of torment where the wicked go at death. The other section of Hades was a place of comfort and hope. This was where all the Old Testament saints went at death. It was not possible for the righteous, who died prior to Christ, to go to Heaven. Christ's blood had not yet been shed for their sins. Therefore they had to wait in the Paradise section of Hades until Christ came for them. Many Bible scholars refer to them as "prisoners of hope." They get this from Isaiah 14:17 where it is written that Satan "opened not the house of his prisoners," or as the marginal reference puts it: "did not let his prisoners loose homewards."

The reason Christ went into Hell (Hades) was to loose these prisoners and take them home to glory. The Bible tells us that at the ascension of Christ our Saviour did indeed release these "prisoners of hope" and take them home to heaven. We find this truth revealed in Eph. 4:8-10 — "When He (Christ) ascended up on high, He led captivity captive," or as the marginal reference has it, "a multitude of captives."

These Old Testament saints were trophies of our Saviour's redeeming grace. When Christ approached the gates of Heaven with these, who are the first fruits of the redeemed, He shouts forth:

> "Lift up your heads O ye gates; and be ye lift up ye everlasting doors; and the King of glory shall come in." (A voice echoes back), "Who is this King of glory?" (Jesus the mighty conqueror answers), "The Lord (Jehovah) strong and mighty, the Lord (Jehovah) mighty in battle — The Lord of hosts, He is the King of glory" (Psalm 24:7-10).

Do you see what it says here? The Bible is speaking of the Lord God Jehovah *who is mighty in battle*. It was Jesus who fought the battle of the ages. It was Jesus who was manifested to destroy the works of the devil (I John 3:8). It was Jesus who conquered death, hell and the grave. It was Jesus who broke the power of sin and set the captives free. Hence it is Jesus who is the Lord God Jehovah mighty in battle. The testimony of scripture cannot be broken: "And without controversy great is the mystery of godliness, *God was manifest in the flesh*" (1 Tim. 3:16). To clinch this great truth, here are the words of the Apostle Paul: "Which none of the princes of this

world knew, for had they known it, they would not have crucified
the Lord of glory" (1 Cor. 2:8).

The one shepherd

The sweet singer of Israel declared, "Jehovah is my shepherd. I
shall lack nothing" (Psalm 23:1, JW Bible). It is strikingly significant
that in John 10:14 Christ declares, "I am the good shepherd, and
know my sheep."

Just who is the good shepherd? Is it Jehovah or Jesus? From the
Christian point of view there is no difference because Jesus of the New
Testament is the Jehovah of the Old Testament. However, one can
readily see that those of the JW persuasion have a real obstacle to overcome here. They cannot dare say there are two good shepherds
because Jesus declares — "there shall be one fold *and one shepherd*"
(John 10:15). If the JW's say that Jehovah is the "one shepherd,"
then they accuse Christ of not speaking the truth when He said,
"I am the good shepherd." They are still in a dilemma even if they
turn about and admit that Christ is the "one shepherd," for then
what will they do with the verse which says, "Jehovah is my shepherd."
It is easy to see here that if the JW's are right and Christ is not God,
then the Bible contradicts itself! It does not matter which way you look
at the JW doctrinal structure, it is simply riddled with such contra-
dictions. Their heretical view that Christ is a creature cannot stand
the acid test of God's Word. They are gored on the horns of a
dilemma here which is of their own making.

Wrong to serve other Gods

"Ye shall not fear other gods, nor bow yourselves to
them, nor serve them, nor sacrifice to them" (2 Kings
17:35).

The Bible commands us here not to *serve* other gods; man is to serve only Jehovah God. Yet Paul tells us, "Ye serve the Lord Jesus" (Col. 3:24). Now if the JW's are right in their teaching on the Person of Christ (and they are not), then there is something decidedly wrong here; for if Christ is "a god," a secondary god, as the JW's teach, *then it would be wrong and sinful to serve Christ* according to 2 Kings 17:35. The only way these two texts can be reconciled is to believe what the Christian Church has always taught, namely that Christ is Almighty God.

Not only is it wrong to *serve* other gods, but our text also tells us that even *bowing* before other gods is forbidden. Yet in Matt. 28:9 we read these words: "And as they (the women) went to tell his disciples, behold Jesus met them saying, all hail. And they came and *held Him by the feet and worshipped Him.*" Here we have the women *bowing* before the feet of the resurrected Christ. Now if Christ is merely some kind of a secondary god as the JW's teach, then these women are guilty of bowing before a god other than Jehovah. Their perverse "a god" fallacy logically leads to this kind of a blasphemous conclusion.

Lord of the elements

When Christ walked our fallen world He proved His Lordship even over the very elements. In Matt. 8:23-27 we have the account of Christ stilling the howling winds and roaring sea. You will recall that in the midst of the storm, the ship in which Jesus and His disciples sailed was in danger of sinking. The disciples were so terrified that they "awoke Him saying, Lord save us; we perish. And He said unto them, Why are ye fearful, O ye of little faith? Then He arose and rebuked the winds and the sea, and there was a great calm. But the men marvelled, saying, *what manner of man is this,* that even the winds and sea obey Him!"

The question asked by the disciples here, which is fraught with wonder and awe, is answered by the Psalmist in these words: "O Lord (Jehovah) of hosts, who is a strong LORD like unto thee? or to thy faithfulness round about thee? Thou (Jehovah) rulest the raging of the sea when the waves thereof arise, thou stillest them" (Psalm 89:8-9). It is clear from this text that the Lord God is the One who rules "the raging of the sea," and who stills the boisterous waves when they arise. Christ therefore proved that He was the Lord God by hushing the howling winds and raging sea to sleep with a word.

Christ further displayed His mastery over the elements by turning water into wine (John 2:9), and by multiplying the loaves and fishes (Matt. 14:19). All physical matter is made up of atoms. Scientists call them the building blocks of the universe. When Christ spoke the atoms obeyed His every command. At the marriage feast Christ spoke to the water and commanded that it should turn into wine. With lightning rapidity the invisible atoms, which made up the water, re-arranged their structure into a different substance called wine. When Christ multiplied the loaves and fishes, myriads of invisible atoms came together and went through such complex maneuvers that their performance would stagger the finite mind. Only the Creator could so order the atoms, the building blocks of the universe, to obey His every command. Oh, the wonder and majesty of it all! Such evidence forces the honest heart to cry out with the prophet of old: "Who is like unto thee, O Lord . . . glorious in holiness, fearful in praise, doing wonders" (Ex. 15:11). Thus Christ is clearly the Lord God because He created all things in heaven and earth (Col. 1:16).

Only God can redeem man

"None of them can by any means redeem his brother,
nor give to God a ransom for him" (Psalm 49:7).

No man, not even a perfect one, has the power to redeem his brother. Only God Almighty can save man. We find this truth stated in Isaiah 43:11. "I, even I, am Jehovah; and beside me there is no saviour" (A.S.V.). The scripture cannot be broken. Jehovah God is the only Saviour. Yet we read in the New Testament that *Christ is the Saviour* (Luke 2:11). If Christ is a creature as the JW's teach, THEN THERE ARE TWO SAVIOURS! The first Saviour would be Jehovah God, and the second Saviour would be an inferior creature saviour called Jesus Christ. We thus see that the JW view concerning Christ as "a god," but not the God, logically leads to a belief in two saviours — an Almighty Saviour and a creature saviour! The thought of such an idea makes one wince. The Trinitarian position avoids this absurd conclusion. True Christians of all ages have ever believed that Jehovah God (the Son) robed Himself in a garment of dust and became man in order to redeem us from the awful penalty of sin.

Christ's enemies were fully aware of the scripture, "I, even I, am Jehovah; and besides me there is no saviour." "I, even I, am he that blotteth out thy transgressions for mine own sake; and will not remember thy sins" (Isa. 43:11, 25). It is clear from this that Christ exercised the prerogative of Deity when He said to the sick of the palsy, "Son, thy sins be forgiven thee" (Mark 2:5). Only God Almighty has the power and the right to forgive sins. The scribes were well aware of this fact; thus they reasoned in their hearts saying, "Why doth this man thus speak blasphemies? Who can forgive sins but God only?" (Mark 2:7). By this one act Christ was saying to His critics, "I am God manifest in the flesh" (1 Tim. 3:16). The JW's will say that the reason Christ could forgive sins was not because He was God, but rather because "the Son of man hath power on earth to forgive sins" (Mark. 2:10). Yes, this is very true. But the reason Christ has power to forgive sins *is because He is God*. If Christ is a creature as the JW's maintain, then it means that a creature can forgive sins! But how can this be so when Jehovah declares that He is the One who forgives men their sins (Isa. 43:25). It should be obvious to anyone with an open mind that Christ is indeed God, for it is only God who can forgive men their sins (Mark 2:7, Isa. 43:25).

Christ is the creator

The JW's teach that Christ is a creature and is therefore part of the order of created things. This false view is exploded by the fact that Col. 1:17 states, "He (Christ) is before all things and by Him all things consist." Since Christ is declared here to be "before all things," He obviously existed before creation and would therefore have to be eternal. Only God could be "before all things." Since this refers to Christ, subsequently our Saviour Jesus Christ is the uncreated and Eternal God.

You will note that Col. 1:17 further tells us, "And by Him (Christ) all things consist." This scripture informs us that "all things" (meaning the universe) consist or are held together by the power of the Son of God. If the JW's are right, then this text teaches that the cosmos is held together by the power of a creature! Scripture teaches that it is only Almighty God who can keep the blazing suns on parade. The "sweet influences of Pleiades" and the "bands of Orion" are held in their respective orbits, not by the power of a creature, but by Almighty God. Yet in the book of Hebrews we learn that it is Christ who is "upholding all things by the word of His power" (Heb. 1.3). In fact the whole context of Col. 1:16-17 portrays Christ, not only as the upholder and sustainer of the universe, BUT AS THE ACTUAL CREATOR OF THE UNIVERSE. The Apostle Paul makes this vividly clear in these words:

> "For by Him (Christ) were all things created, that are
> in heaven, and that are in earth, visible and invisible,
> whether they be thrones, or dominions, or principalities,
> or powers: all things were created by Him and for Him"
> (Col. 1:16).

If the JW's are right and Christ is not God but merely a creature, then this scripture teaches THAT A CREATURE CREATED THE UNIVERSE. Just think of it! All things in heaven and earth *were created by a creature*. What blasphemous conclusions their error laden teachings lead to.

Our text not only tells us that all things were created by Christ, but also "for Him" (Col. 1:16). If the JW's are correct, then this can only mean that all things in heaven and earth were created for a creature. This will be a bitter pill for JW's to swallow. Nevertheless their teaching that Christ is a creature logically leads to the heretical conclusion that all things in heaven and earth were created by a creature and for a creature. Such a view is too absurd for words. Holy Writ clearly teaches that it is for the Eternal God that all things were created. Hear what the scriptures saith: "For thou (Jehovah) hast created all things, and for thy pleasure they are and were created" (Rev. 4:11). The Bible tells us here that it is for the pleasure of Jehovah that all things are created. Hence Christ is Jehovah God (the Son), the One for whom all things in heaven and earth were created.

Christ is eternal

The Witnesses deny the eternal existence of the Son of God. They erroneously teach there was a time when the Son of God had no existence. Such a view is false and utterly contrary to the teaching of the Bible as the following will show.

We read in Heb. 1:3 that the Son is declared to be "the brightness of His (the Father's) glory." If there was a time when the Son did not exist, then there was also a time when the brightness of the Father's glory did not exist. To deny the eternal existence of the Son of God is to also deny the eternal existence of *the brightness of the Father's glory*. You cannot have one without the other. Thus even the Father's glory is brought into question by this JW heresy.

The Apostle Paul makes this tremendous claim concerning Christ: "But unto them which are called, both Jews and Greeks, *Christ the power of God and the wisdom of God"* (1 Cor. 1:24). Note that Christ is called "the power and wisdom of God." This text finds the chink in the Arian armour. For if there was a time when the Son of God did not exist, then there was also a time when THE POWER AND WISDOM OF GOD DID NOT EXIST! Surely it is obvious that since "the power and wisdom of God" is eternal, then Christ also must be eternal *because He is the power and wisdom of God.*

The Bible declares, "In the beginning was the Word (Christ), and the Word was with God, and the Word was God" (John 1:1). We are told here that the Word was "In the beginning with God (the Father)." Since the Word was there "In the beginning," the Word then existed BEFORE THE START OF THE BEGINNING. Thus Christ, the Word, is outside the order of creation and is therefore uncreated and eternal.

In Isaiah 9:6 the child born and the Son given is called "the Everlasting Father," or as Young's Literal Translation puts it, "Father of Eternity." This is not to say that Christ is God the Father. The term "father" is sometimes used in the Bible figuratively. We read where the Jews said, "Abraham is our father" (John 8:39). Actually Abraham had only eight sons. But it was through Abraham that the Jewish nation came into being. When the Bible speaks of Christ as being the "Father of Eternity," it is saying that Christ is the Creator of everything that comprises eternity. The lowly babe in Bethlehem's manger fathered the universe. How can this One not be God? The all pervading power of the Crucified "Lord of Glory" originally welded the cosmos together. This is why Isaiah calls the Christ Child not only the Father of Eternity, but also "The Mighty God." The faithful dupes of this Christ-denying Watchtower system are forced to stand condemned as shameless deceivers before such revelation of truth.

Principle of exception

Concerning Christ we read, "All things were made by Him and without Him was not anything made that was made" (John 1:3). This text informs us that Christ created everything that was ever created. Hence Christ is God seeing that He is the Creator of everything that was ever created (Gen. 1:1). The JW's are forced by the authority of this text to the ridiculous conclusion that if Christ was created — THEN HE MUST HAVE CREATED HIMSELF! To believe that the Father created the Son is to deny this text which declares, "WITHOUT HIM WAS NOT ANYTHING MADE THAT WAS MADE." This false JW teaching that the Father created the Son has been tested by scripture here and is shown to have a major flaw in it.

The attempt of Witnesses to get around this text would be laughable if it were not so serious. During one of their big District Watchtower Conventions held in Vancouver, the writer had the opportunity to discuss the Bible with a JW couple from California. The man was extremely well versed in Watchtower theology. He was articulate, polite, soft spoken, well dressed, and as I remember, always smiling. Our JW opponent had all the characteristics of a cracker-jack salesman.

During our discussion this very text of John 1:3 was raised by the writer to prove that Christ is eternal. After we had expounded this scripture (as in the above), the JW replied by throwing us this curve. He asked us, "Have you ever heard of the 'principle of the exception'?" We replied that to our knowledge such a thing didn't exist in the Bible. Our smiling JW then deftly opened his Bible and read: "And call no man your father upon the earth; for one is your Father, which is in heaven" (Matt. 23:9). Our JW friend then pointed out that we can call our earthly father, "father," and yet not disobey this scriptural command. He then argued that this proves there is an exception built into this text even though it is not mentioned. "Here is the principle of the exception," he said.

The JW then took his so-called "principle of the exception" and applied it to our proof text of John 1:3. You will recall that this text reads, "All things were made by Him (Christ) and without Him was not anything made that was made." Armed with his "principle of the exception," this Watchtower conjurer began explaining away our proof text. He admitted this scripture proves that all things that were ever made were created by Christ. Yet he animately proclaimed that when you apply the "principle of the exception" here, it becomes obvious that Christ is the one exception. In other words, we are asked to believe that our text does not really mean that "without Him (Christ) was not anything made that was made." For we have just been told here that Christ is the exception.

We must give the devil his due. This is certainly a very ingenious method of explaining away scriptures which contradict their point of view. We were momentarily stunned by such a dazzling display of scripture manipulation. After a moment's reflection we felt led to ask this polished deceiver the following questions: Where does this so-called "principle of the exception" begin and where does it end? Since you promiscuously use this "principle" as an escape hatch in order to avoid being pinned down by scripture, how do you feel about applying it to the following scriptural command: "Thou shalt not steal" (Ex. 20:15). Who is the exception here? Still another good example reads: "Thou shalt not commit adultery" (Ex. 20:14). I wonder whom we might name as being the exception here? At this point in our conversation the JW's wife began to snicker and laugh.

Even she could see just how ridiculous their so-called "principle of the exception" looks under scriptural analysis.

We have submitted this incident to show what lengths JW's will go in order to empty the scriptures of their real meaning. Their impious imaginings and blasphemous assertions rise up as a stench in the nostrils of the Lord God. You can pile up truth after truth before their very eyes and still they will reject it. The twisted contortions which these deceivers will go through reveal their ingrained prejudice and hatred for the truth. The devotees of this cult are unscrupulous tricksters who will resort to bold and reckless misuse of the scriptures to accomplish their purpose. Regardless of all the elusive tactics ever devised by these deceivers, they can never alter God's unerring Word. It is written: "Forever, O Lord, thy Word is settled in heaven" (Psalm 119:89).

Father and Son are co-equal

"All men should honour the Son even as they honour the Father" (John 5:23).

These words are positive proof that Christ claimed equal honour with the Father. In our text the word "even" comes from the Greek KATHOS and literally means "according as" (Young's Concordance). In other words all men are commanded to "honour the Son ACCORDING AS they honour the Father." But do the JW's obey this command of scripture? No, they certainly do not believe that Christ is to receive the same honour as the Father. One wonders how they justify themselves here in the light of their own Bible which reads, "All may honour the Son just as they honour the Father."

The Witnesses claim to honour the Father by worshipping Him; yet their own Bible tells them here to "honour the Son just as they honour the Father." But do they worship Christ? We have learned in this book that the JW's certainly do not worship Christ. The followers of the Watchtower cult say they honour the Father by acknowledging Him as Almighty God. Why don't they also acknowledge the Son as Almighty God? Their own Bible tells them to "honour the Son just as they honour the Father." This is added Biblical proof that the JW's do indeed belittle Christ.

To anyone whose mind has not been warped by prejudice and blindness, the words of our text explicitly show that Christ claimed EQUAL HONOUR WITH GOD THE FATHER. Peddlers of Watchtower error would do well to remember that it would be sheer blasphemy for any creature to solemnly announce that he is to be honoured *just as the Eternal Father is honoured!* Only one who was equal with God the Father could rightfully make such a claim as this and not be guilty of gross blasphemy.

Another scripture which delivers a crushing blow to this Christ-belittling System is John 16:15. "All things that the Father hath are mine." This is indeed a tremendous claim. Christ is saying here that He possesses all the titles and attributes which belong to God the Father. Since the Father is Almighty, then Christ too is Almighty, because everything that the Father possesses is also His. You say that the Father is eternal — likewise the Son is eternal. To say this is false is to accuse Christ of speaking a lie because He said, "All things that the Father hath are mine." There is not one thing any JW can name belonging to the Father which Christ does not also possess. We challenge them to find one. They cannot do so. For Christ stops them cold in their heretical tracks when He declares, "ALL THINGS THAT THE FATHER HATH ARE MINE." What creature could dare make such a claim? It would be treason and blasphemy for Christ to make this claim if He were not truly co-equal with the Eternal Father.

Equal in power and glory

Christ is unquestionably co-equal with the Father because just prior to His ascension into Heaven He made this claim: "All power is given unto Me in heaven and in earth" (Matt. 28:18). Notice the fact that Christ has all power in Heaven. To have all power is to have *omnipotence.* Only Almighty God has *omnipotence.* Hence Christ is Almighty God because He said He possessed *omnipotence.* Surely it would be sacrilegious for any creature to make such a claim. Since

Christ has all power in Heaven and earth, He is therefore co-equal with the Father. If this is not true, then words do not mean what they say.

The JW's will quickly point out from our text that Christ has been "given" all power. They maintain that since Christ was "given" all power, there must have been a time when He didn't have all power. Hence He could not be God. Their argument here is invalid and has no basis in scripture as we shall shortly see. Assuming that the JW's are right on this point (and they are not), the fact remains THAT CHRIST NOW HAS ALL POWER IN HEAVEN AND EARTH. From the JW point of view this can only mean that a creature has been elevated into the Godhead and given equal power with Almighty God! Just think of it! According to the JW's there is now a creature in Heaven equal in power with Almighty God. The JW's can fume and froth all they want, but this fact is undeniable — CHRIST NOW HAS ALL POWER IN HEAVEN AND EARTH. Consequently if Christ is but a creature as they falsely teach, then a creature is now equal in power with Jehovah God. This is one festering, heretical blemish they will never be able to cover over.

That facet of their argument that declares Christ could not be God (because He has been given all power) is equally as fallacious as the idea that a mere creature now has all power in Heaven and earth. The fact that Christ was "given" all power (after His Resurrection) in no way detracts from His inherent Deity. You will recall that in John 17:5 Jesus prayed: "O Father, glorify thou me with thine own self with the glory which I had with thee before the world was." Power and glory are interwoven. Thus when Christ came into our fallen world, He laid aside the glory which He shared with the Father before the worlds were made. After His Resurrection the Son receives back the glory which He originally shared with the Father. Thus Christ could rightly say after His Resurrection — "All power is given unto Me in heaven and in earth."

The JW's would like to make out that this is the first time the Son ever had all power. Nowhere does the Bible say such a thing. The fact that Christ shared the Father's glory "before the world was" is clear proof that in eternity past He was co-equal with the Father. It is also abundantly clear that when Christ prayed, "O Father, glorify thou Me with thine own self with the glory I had with thee *before the world was*," that He was laying claim to a pre-existence that goes beyond the foundations of the world. According to Gen. 1:1 our earth was created when the universe was created — "In the beginning." Beyond the other side of the "beginning" is eternity. Christ clearly claimed an existence "before the world was"; hence even before the beginning of the created universe. Consequently the Son of God has an eternal, everlasting, unbegun existence and is therefore co-equal with the Father (Micah 5:2).

Christ further teaches that He is co-equal with the Father when He invites the troubled and weary to put their faith and trust in Him. Listen to our Lord's gracious words: "Come unto Me, all ye that labour and are heavy laden, and I will give you rest" (Matt. 11:28). Notice that Christ invites them to come unto Himself, for He is the One who will give them rest. If Christ is not truly God, then Christians of all ages have put their faith *in a creature!* Consider the implications of this statement. It would mean that the head of the Church is not God, *but a creature!* Oh, the blasphemy of it!

The Apostle Paul bears witness to the great truth of Christ's Deity when he declares — "For in Him (Christ) dwelleth all the fulness of the Godhead bodily" (Col. 2:9). The Greek term for "Godhead" is THEOTETOS and literally means — DEITY. Accordingly Moffatt's translation renders this verse, "For it is in him that all the fulness of the Deity dwells bodily." In other words all the fulness of Deity dwells in Christ bodily. The JW's in their Bible pervert this great text by rendering the term "Godhead" (or Deity) as merely "the divine quality." This JW expression "the divine quality" really means nothing, for all men have a divine quality about them since they are a creation of God. By boldly mistranslating this text they thus rob Christ of His Deity. The JW's are hard put to find even one authority to back up their watered down translation of this great text. The dishonest translators of the JW Bible thus pit themselves against the best scholarship of all ages. For example, Thayer's "Greek-English Lexicon of the New Testament" (page 288) states that THEOTETOS (Godhead, Deity) means "i.e., the state of being God, Godhead" (Col. 2:9). If Christ is not God, then a creature has been lifted into the Godhead and given all the fullness of Deity! Such an absurdity provides its own disproof.

The weight of evidence proving the Holy Trinity and the Deity of Christ is crushing and conclusive. These two great doctrines are central pillars in the Christian Faith. It has been shown throughout these pages that the Trinity and Christ's Deity are supported by a wall of absolute impregnable scriptural evidence. These great truths are woven into the very core and fiber of Holy Scripture. The ingenious trickery and wilful perversions employed by JW's against the Divine Record have been laid bare here for all to see. We have demonstrated how they will deliberately invent lie after lie to get around scriptures that expose their blasphemous errors. The cult of which we speak is clearly one of the Devil's twentieth century counterfeit missionary movements.

Chapter six

THE RESURRECTION OF CHRIST

The Bodily Resurrection of Christ is also denied by the JW's. In his book, "The Time Is At Hand" p. 129, Pastor Russell makes this statement:

> "Our Lord's human body was, however, supernaturally removed from the tomb . . . Whether it was dissolved into gases or whether it is still preserved somewhere as a grand memorial of God's love . . . no one knows." The JW's further declare, "Jesus' Resurrection Not of Same Body: He merely Materialized Flesh and Blood to be Seen and Believed" (Make Sure Of All Things, p. 314, 1953 Edition).

Such statements are indeed damnable lies. You will recall the disciples told the Apostle Thomas that they had seen the Risen Lord. Doubting Thomas replies: "Except I shall see in His hands the print of the nails, and put my fingers into the print of the nails, and thrust my hand into His side, I will not believe" (John 20:25). Some days later Jesus appears to Thomas and invites him to inspect the nail prints in His hands and feet, and also the spear wound in His side. Beholding the Risen Saviour, Thomas believes and cries out to Jesus: "My Lord and my God" (John 20:28).

Thus the Bible clearly shows that Christ did indeed rise from the dead bodily. In a vain attempt to save face here the JW's will unblushingly declare that Christ simply materialized on this occasion a body quite similar to the one that was crucified. This is mere speculation on their part and has not one shred of scriptural support. Only those whose minds are utterly infested with error could possibly accept such blasphemous speculation.

Let us not forget the words of the Apostle Thomas: "Except I put my finger into the print of the nails — I will not believe." Thomas had to behold the real crucified Body of Christ before he would believe the Lord was risen. He insisted upon seeing *the real marks* of the nail prints and spear thrust. Any so-called materialized body certainly would not have NAIL PRINTS THAT WERE MADE BY REAL NAILS! The JW's would have us believe that Christ here was some sort of clever trickster who went around producing fake nail prints and spear wounds in various materialized bodies. This is merely another example of the way they pervert and distort Holy Scripture.

On still another occasion Jesus said to His disciples, "Behold *my hands and my feet,* that it is I myself, handle Me and see; for a spirit hath not flesh and bones as ye see Me have" (Luke 24:39). The phrase "my hands and my feet" denotes personal possession. Consequently the body Christ was here showing to His disciples was most certainly His own crucified Body. If this were merely a "materialized body" (as the JW's affirm), then Christ did not really own it. For this so-called "materialized body" was (according to JW's) only produced or borrowed for the occasion.

If Christ displayed to the disciples merely a materialized body, then He was inviting them to inspect a body that contained *make believe wounds!* From the JW point of view this can only mean that Christ is saying to the disciples, "Behold THE FAKE WOUNDS in my hands and my feet, that it is I myself . . ." Their denial of the Bodily Resurrection of Christ logically leads to the profane conclusion that Christ here is out to hoodwink the disciples. It becomes painfully clear that if Christ is showing His disciples a DIFFERENT BODY, other than the one crucified, then Christ would be guilty of producing false evidence to prove His resurrection. The very fact that Christ invites His disciples to examine His hands and feet is positive proof that He was showing them the actual body that bore the awful wounds of Calvary.

Objections

The JW's have several stock arguments against the Bodily Resurrection of Christ. First of all they will say that Christ was not raised bodily because Paul said, "Flesh and blood cannot inherit the kingdom of God" (1 Cor. 15:50). What they refuse to consider is that the phrase "flesh and blood" appears four times in the New Testament, and in each instance can only mean natural man. The following evidence will confirm our claim. You will recall that Jesus said unto Peter, "Blessed art thou, Simon Barjona: for *flesh and blood* hath not revealed it unto thee, but my Father which is in heaven" (Matt. 16:13-17). Surely Christ is not referring here to literal flesh and blood, but rather to natural man. The third instance is when Paul states, "For we wrestle not against *flesh and blood*, but against principalities and powers . . ." (Eph. 6:12). The phrase "flesh and blood" is again clearly figurative, meaning natural man. Our fourth example where this term appears reads as follows: "I conferred not with *flesh and blood*" (Gal. 1:16). How could Paul possibly confer (talk things over) with LITERAL FLESH AND LITERAL BLOOD? Surely it is obvious what Paul means here. He is saying, "I conferred not with NATURAL MAN." Consequently the reason "flesh and blood" (natural man) cannot inherit the kingdom of God is because natural man needs to be born again (John 3:3). Christ's blood (the life force of His natural body) was shed for the sins of the world. When Christ rose from the dead a new life force permeated His glorified fleshly Body, namely the Spirit of God.

In the spirit

In their determined attempt to discredit the Bodily Resurrection of Christ, the JW's will also quote Peter who speaks of Christ "being put to death in the flesh, but being made alive in the Spirit" (1 Peter 3:18, JW Bible). They argue that this means Christ was raised from the dead a spirit creature. But nowhere does it say here (or anywhere else) that Christ was raised a spirit. This text simply informs us that Christ was raised *in the spirit*. Now if the JW's are right and this expression "in the spirit" means to be a spirit creature, then all the living Christians in Rome during Paul's day were spirit creatures!

Why? Because Paul wrote to them these words: "'Ye are not in the flesh, but in the spirit" (Rom. 8:9). Likewise the Apostle John must have also been a spirit creature when he wrote the book of Revelation. You will recall that John said, "I was in the Spirit on the Lord's day" (Rev. 1:10). Surely John did not mean to infer that he was a spirit creature on the Lord's day. Nor was Paul trying to tell the living Christians at Rome that they were spirit creatures because they were in the spirit. When Christians are "in the spirit," it means they are controlled by the Spirit of God. The JW argument that "in the spirit" means to be a spirit creature is thus shown to be nonsensical.

It is certainly true that Christ was made alive "in the spirit." However, this does not mean that Christ was raised a spirit, but rather that the Spirit of God raised up Jesus even as it is written: "But if the Spirit of Him that has raised up Jesus from among the dead dwell in you . . ." (Rom. 8:11). We thus see that 1 Peter 3:18 does not teach that Christ was raised a spirit creature. This verse is simply telling us that Christ was raised by the Spirit of God.

Why Christ was not recognized

There are three accounts given in scripture where Jesus was not immediately recognized after His Resurrection. The JW's seize upon these three instances to try and disprove the Bodily Resurrection of Christ. They maintain that since Jesus was not immediately recognized, He therefore did not appear in the same body in which He had lived and was crucified, but instead created different bodies as the occasion demanded. According to the JW's, Christ would materialize a body for a specific occasion, and when the task for which He had created this particular body was completed, He would then dissolve this materialized body back into the elements from which He had made it. When the occasion would again occur where Christ needed a body, He would just simply materialize another new body, then dispose of it, and so on. Nor is this all. The worst is yet to come. According to these "profound Bible scholars", our Risen Lord played the role of a quick-switch artist. Here are the words of the founder of this cult:

"The power manifested by our Lord and the angels to create and *dissolve the clothing in which they appeared,* was just as superhuman as the creating and dissolving of their assumed human bodies: and the bodies were no more their glorious spiritual bodies than were the clothes they wore." Again, "The clothing in which He appeared on the occasions mentioned *must have been specially created,* and probably was the most appropriate for each occasion. For instance, when He appeared as a gardener to Mary, it was probably *in such apparel as a gardener would wear"* (Studies in the Scriptures, Vol. 2, pp. 127-128).

Have you ever beheld such a putrid batch of impious guesses and blasphemous assertions! Untold numbers have been duped by the vain imaginings of these deceivers. There is not a shred of scriptural proof to back up their wild claim that Christ ever appeared in *a series of different materialized bodies.* Neither is there any scriptural evidence to support their incredible absurdity that each materialized body was clothed WITH SPECIALLY CREATED APPAREL "most appropriate for each occasion."

Notice what they say about Christ appearing to Mary. They tell us that our Lord "appeared as a gardener to Mary." This is another example of their scripture twisting. For the Bible plainly relates that it was a mistake on the part of Mary. "She *supposing* Him to be the gardener" is the way the Bible Record reads (John 20:15). The mistake on Mary's part is quite understandable when one considers the fact that she was grief stricken. Neither should we forget that "Mary came very early in the morning while it was yet dark" (John 20:1). Surely this suggests that the tomb must have been rather dark. When we consider all the circumstances of this account, it should be easy to understand why Mary *"supposed* Him to be the gardener." But the Witnesses do not want to accept this evidence. They would have us believe that Christ was a clever impersonator of various characters, and that He was using sleight of hand trickery to deceive people into believing that He was the very same Jesus.

The second instance when the Risen Lord was not immediately

recognized by His disciples is found in John 21:4-12. This account relates that Jesus stood on the sea shore while the disciples were out on the water in a ship. When we consider the fact that morning had just dawned, and take into account also the distance between the Lord and His disciples, it should be understandable why the disciples did not immediately recognize Jesus.

The third time the Risen Lord was not immediately recognized took place when He appeared to the two disciples on the Emmaus road. Actually the scriptures teach that Christ didn't want these two disciples to immediately recognize Him, for He wanted to test their faith. This is clearly evident by the fact that the Bible declares, "But their eyes were holden that they should not know Him" (Luke 24:16).

We are thus told that by an act of Divine power, Christ supernaturally closed the disciples' eyes so that they should not recognize Him. This by itself clearly proves that Christ must have risen from the dead in the very same body in which the disciples were accustomed to seeing Him before His Resurrection. Else why would it be necessary for their eyes to be holden that they should not know Him? The only honest answer has to be that if they had beheld Christ as He really was, then they would have known that the stranger who was walking beside them that day was indeed the very same Jesus whom they knew so well. The account goes on to say that after Christ had tested their faith, "Their eyes were opened and they knew Him" (Luke 24:31).

We have given sound scriptural reasons why Christ was not immediately recognized on these three particular occasions after His Resurrection. The JW's will stubbornly refuse to accept our scriptural answers to their false charge that Christ appeared in different materialized bodies. Regardless of all the evidence against them, they will still continue to parrot the Watchtower lie that these three appearances (in which the Risen Christ was not immediately recognized) still prove that Christ materialized different bodies.

Blinded by their own prejudice and hatred of the truth, they fail to see the main weakness in their false theory that the Resurrected Christ appeared in different materialized bodies. For if what they say is true, then this means that each and every time Christ was not immediately recognized by His disciples is proof that He must have had a different body. It is precisely at this point that the trap is sprung which catches them in their own lie. You will recall that the Bible tells us in Matt. 14:26 that Christ walked on the water, and His disciples MISTOOK Him for a spirit. To be consistent the JW's will have to believe that this incident also shows that Christ must have materialized a different body. Why? Because His disciples failed to recognize Christ as He walked on the water. We thus see that the false teaching of the JW's that Christ must have materialized different bodies (because His disciples failed to recognize Him on three occasions) explodes in their own faces. For this appearance of Christ took place BEFORE HIS CRUCIFIXION! Not even the JW's would be so foolish as to say that Christ materialized different bodies BEFORE HIS CRUCIFIXION!

It is glaringly evident that the JW's base their teaching of the "different materialized bodies" of Christ on mere assumption and not on scriptural fact. We challenge any JW to show us just one scripture which states that Christ materialized a physical body to prove to His disciples that He had risen from the dead. There is no such scripture; furthermore they know it.

Their view is absurd

It is ridiculous for JW's to say they believe in the Resurrection of Christ. How can they honestly claim to believe this great truth when they deny the Resurrection of the Crucified Body of Christ? For the JW's to dare talk of believing in the Resurrection of Christ, after putting forth the statements they have, is an insult to intelligence. It would be well for them to take note of the fact that it was Christ's Crucified Body that was laid in the tomb, and it was the absence of that Crucified Body from the tomb which caused the angel to announce — "He is not here, He is risen" (Luke 24:6). Please note that the angel does not say anything here about Christ's Body being "dissolved into gases," as the founder of the Watchtower cult has blasphemously suggested. Nor does the angel announce that Christ was raised *merely a spirit*. But what the angel does proclaim is the glorious truth that *"He is risen."*

The word "He" is a simple pronoun denoting the total person. When we say of someone, "He came to dinner last night," we are talking about someone who came and bodily sat down to dinner. When John's little playmate comes knocking at the door and says to mother, "Is Johnny still in bed?" and mother replies, "He is risen," immediately that little five year old knows that Johnny is bodily out of bed. But JW's do not have the honesty and innocence of little children. When they are shown what the angel said on Resurrection morning, "He is not here; He is risen," they will immediately balk and resort to devices of every kind in order to undermine the truth of Christ's Bodily Resurrection. Watchtower double talk is one of the tricks employed by these deceivers to pervert the Divine Record concerning Christ's Bodily Resurrection. By allowing their imagination to run amuck, they can warp the scriptures to fit almost any wild theory. Oh, the souls that have been blinded by this false system of religion. Surely this cult is one of the greatest frauds ever perpetrated on humanity.

The climax of absurdity

If according to the JW's the crucified body of Jesus was not resurrected from the dead, then perhaps they can tell us what part of Jesus was raised from the dead? It could not have been His soul, for the Witnesses maintain that man does not possess a soul separate and distinct from the body. This, therefore, rules out any possibility of Christ's soul being resurrected apart from His body. We are now left only with Christ's human spirit. But the JW's tell us that man's spirit is not an intelligent entity. The spirit of man is said by the JW's to be only his breath, something windlike, or his mental disposition. (Make Sure Of All Things, page 357.)

The only conclusion one can come to after examining their view is that the JW's are forced to believe that only Christ's spirit was resurrected. But when we consider their interpretation of the term "spirit," this can only mean from their point of view that IT WAS JUST CHRIST'S BREATH OR MENTAL DISPOSITION THAT WAS RESURRECTED!

How ridiculous! How absurd! Their own twisted logic has again trapped them.

Another dogmatic statement of error which issues from this same poison fountain declares that the human spirit "does not produce intelligence apart from the physical body."* The text which they use to support this false claim is Psalm 146:4. Needless to say, they misapply this text to make it mean that at death the human spirit has no consciousness or intelligence. In their blind zeal to push this point, they leave themselves open to a devastating blow from which they will never recover. For if the human spirit (as they state) "does not produce intelligence apart from the physical body," then this can only mean that the Christ of the JW's, who supposedly was raised a spirit, had no intelligence! By their own declaration the spirit risen jesus of the Watchtower is thus devoid of intelligence and is therefore an idiot. The JW's may howl and scream all they want, but the fact remains that if Christ was raised from the dead WITHOUT HIS PHYSICAL BODY (as they falsely teach), then the jesus they believe in has to be an idiot! For according to their own words the spirit "does not produce intelligence apart from the physical body."

Further proofs

There is one text which soundly rebukes this false system for their denial of the Bodily Resurrection of Christ. Here it is. "For there is one God, and one Mediator between God and men, the *man* Christ Jesus" (1 Tim. 2:5). The one Mediator between God and men is not "a spirit creature," but the MAN Christ Jesus. Even the JW's must admit that a man is one who has a body. Therefore the MAN Christ Jesus, who is now in Heaven, has a glorified human body. Christ's natural body was put to death on the Cross, but it (the natural body) was quickened and raised a glorified spiritual body. What we are saying is that on Resurrection Morning a spiritual life force animated the crucified body of Christ making it immortal.

---

* "Make Sure Of All Things," p.466

The JW's further argue that Christ was not raised bodily because He appeared to the disciples in the upper room when "the doors were shut" (John 20:26). We answer this by pointing out that Christ had a "spiritual body" (1 Cor. 15:50). With His glorified Resurrection body Christ could transcend the physical laws of the universe at will. Consequently Christ could command the atoms, which made up His glorified physical body, to separate and go through walls and then reassemble themselves together on the other side.

Another argument put forth by the Witnesses is that Christ could not have taken back His body after paying the ransom price for sin. To do so, they say, would nullify the ransom. Their claim here is most unsound because if what they say is true, then the fact that Christ took back his life would also make the ransom null and void. Did not Jesus say, "I lay down my life that I might take it again — I have power to lay it down, and I have power to take it again" (John 10:17-18).

Christ's body was resurrected

Let the following words of scripture forever sweep aside their blasphemous denial of our Lord's Bodily Resurrection. Here they are:

> "Jesus answered and said unto them, Destroy this temple and in three days I will raise it up. Then said the Jews, Forty and six years was this temple in building, and wilt thou rear it up in three days? But He spake of THE TEMPLE OF HIS BODY" (John 2:19-23).

The JW's will try to squirm out from under this embarrassing text in the following evasive manner. They will say, "Christ here was only speaking in a figurative sense concerning His spiritual body — the Church!" The fatal defect in this piece of scripture twisting is the fact that Christ here is clearly talking about A BODY THAT THE JEWS COULD DESTROY OR KILL. Certainly the Jews could not destroy or kill Christ's spiritual body, the Church. This is evident by the fact that our Saviour said, "The gates of hell shall not prevail against the Church" (Matt. 16:18). It is therefore crystal clear that Christ here is talking about HIS PHYSICAL BODY which the Jews could and did destroy by crucifixion. But in three days Christ fulfilled His promise and raised the temple of His body up again.

The proof just submitted strikingly demonstrates the venomous error contained in this damnable system. We have confronted JW's time and time again with this evidence, and not one of them has ever been able to answer it. When you press JW's to give a reason why they aren't able to answer this proof text, they will give you the lame excuse that the rank and file DON'T HAVE ALL THE ANSWERS! However, they quickly assure us that our questions can be easily answered by the Society, if we will just write them. Poor blinded dupes! Can't they think for themselves? The Society cannot answer, any more than they can, the evidence contained in John 2:19-22 substantiating the all-important doctrine of the Bodily Resurrection of Christ.

In all the countless magazines and books published by this cult, never once, to our knowledge, has the Society ever attempted to answer the proofs we have just submitted from John 2:19-22, which so clearly establish the Bodily Resurrection of Christ. The Watchtower leaders are astute enough to know that the evidence found in John 2:19-22 is a damning indictment against them. This is undoubtedly the reason they have adopted an attitude of silence concerning this great text. For this scripture, more than any other, proves that JW's do not really believe in the Resurrection of Christ.

Still another proof that Christ was raised bodily from the dead are His own words to Mary on Resurrection Morning: "Touch Me not, for I am not yet ascended to my Father" (John 20:17). The words of our Lord here can only mean that He was going to ascend into Heaven with the same body with which He appeared to Mary. OTHER-WISE WHY DID JESUS FORBID MARY HERE TO TOUCH HIM? It would be impossible for Mary to touch Christ's spirit. It seems clear that Christ must have first ascended to the Father between the time He appeared to Mary and the time He showed Himself to His disciples in the upper room. Obviously by this time Christ had already presented Himself to the Father because now He says to the disciples — "Handle Me and see, for a spirit hath not flesh and bones, as ye see Me have" (Luke 24:39). Christ's final ascension to the Father took place some forty days after His resurrection.

Here is another text which affords conclusive proof for the Bodily Resurrection of Christ: "For David speaketh concerning Him (Christ), I foresaw the Lord always before my face, for He is on my right hand, that I should not be moved. Therefore did my heart rejoice, and my tongue was glad; moreover also MY FLESH SHALL REST IN HOPE. Because thou wilt not leave my soul in hell, neither wilt thou suffer thine Holy One to see corruption" (Acts 2:25-27).

This portion of scripture is admitted by all (JW's included) to be a prophecy concerning Christ's Resurrection. Notice what our text says here about Christ's body: "ALSO MY FLESH SHALL REST IN HOPE." What was Christ's flesh to rest in hope of here? Was Christ's flesh to rest in hope of being "dissolved into gases," as the founder of the Watchtower has suggested? Absurd! The context clearly reveals that Christ's flesh was to rest in hope of a resurrection. It is written: "Because thou (Father) wilt not leave my soul in hell, neither wilt thou suffer thine Holy One to see *corruption*" (Acts 2:27). Once again the JW's are weighed in the balance and found wanting.

Let us not forget Rom. 8:11 which states, "But if the Spirit of Him that raised up Jesus from the dead dwell in you, He that raised up Christ shall ALSO quicken your MORTAL BODIES." This term "also" presupposes that Christ has had His mortal body quickened or resurrected. Some glorious day Christ also "shall change our vile body, that it may be fashioned like unto His glorious body" (Phil. 3:21).

The JW's will try and slide around this last text by saying that Paul here is not referring to our physical bodies being changed like unto Christ's glorious physical body. Oh, no! They tell us that Paul here is actually talking about the body of Christ — the Church — that will one day be made glorious. Their attempt to twist this text is checked by the fact that Paul says "OUR BODY." The word "our" denotes personal possession. The Bible never speaks of the Church as the body of the saints. The Church is always called Christ's body. Neither is the Church ever spoken of as "OUR VILE BODY." Therefore it is our vile physical bodies that shall be "fashioned like unto His glorious body."

In concluding our thoughts on this great theme, let us remember Rom. 8:23 — "We ourselves groan within ourselves, waiting for the adoption, to wit, THE REDEMPTION OF OUR BODY." The scriptures thus clearly show that it is our personal physical bodies that shall be redeemed from the grave. The Apostle Paul's main theme was that Christ died to redeem man. All will admit that the body of man *is part of man*. Hence Christ died to redeem the whole man. If the JW's are right and the body of man is not to be redeemed, then this means that Christ died to redeem ONLY A PART OF MAN! But where does it state in scripture that Christ died to redeem ONLY A PART OF MAN?

We would ask the JW's this question concerning the Resurrection of Christ. Where does it say in scripture THAT ONLY A PART OF CHRIST WAS RESURRECTED? Let us consider this text. "When they had fulfilled all that was written of Him, they took Him down from the tree, and laid Him in a sepulchre, BUT GOD RAISED HIM FROM THE DEAD" (Acts 13:29-30). Words could not make it any clearer. It was the body of Christ that was laid in the sepulchre. Therefore it was the body of Christ that was raised from the dead.

The JW's may think they believe in the Resurrection of Christ. But the evidence submitted in these pages clearly shows that they are entangled in the worst kind of error. To deny what the Bible teaches concerning Christ's Resurrection is to be forever lost and eternally damned. It is written:

"That if thou shalt confess with thy mouth the Lord
Jesus, and shalt believe in thine heart that God hath raised
Him from the dead, thou shalt be saved" (Rom. 10:9).

The JW's do not believe in their hearts that God has raised Jesus *bodily* from the dead as the scriptures teach; therefore how can those who die as JW's ever be saved? The soul destroying heresies of this accursed cult will damn them to Hell. Those who propagate the pernicious errors of this damnable system may well tremble, for they will find to their awful dismay that it was not the truth they had embraced; rather it was a soul consuming curse which they had accepted into their bosom.

Chapter seven

THE GREAT FARCE

Pastor Russell, founder of the Watchtower, prophesied that our churches, schools, banks, and governments would be completely destroyed by October of 1914. Hear the mouthings of this false prophet concerning God's Kingdom:

> "Its influence and work will result in the complete destruction of 'the powers that be' of 'this present evil world,' political, financial, ecclesiastical . . . by the close of the times of the Gentiles, October, A.D. 1914" (Millennial Dawn, Vol. 4, page 622). On page 99 Vol. 2, Russell further says — "The final end of the kingdoms of this world, and the full establishment of the kingdom of God, will be accomplished by the end of A.D. 1914."

Please note that in these prophecies the words COMPLETE, FINAL END, AND FULL ESTABLISHMENT do not permit them to change the dates for the fulfillment of these prophecies. However in a later edition of these books showing the publisher's date of 1923 the words "by the close" in the first prophecy are changed to "about the close." Likewise in the second prophecy the words "by the end," are changed to "near the end." It has been well said, "Even with these changes the fulfillment is long overdue."

In Volume 7 of Russell's books the collapse of the world is postponed for four years! All JW's were told at that time: "In the year 1918, when God destroys the churches wholesale and the church members by millions, it shall be that any that escape shall come to the works of Pastor Russell (not Judge Rutherford or JW's of today) to learn the meaning of the downfall of Christianity" (Vol. 7, p. 485).

It appears from this that the survivors (whether they like it or not) will be the very thing they declare themselves not to be — *Russellites!* It must have been a bitter pill for Russell to swallow when the happenings of 1914 mocked his soothsayings. Instead of a Millennial Paradise, the peoples of the earth were thrown into a World War. The grim irony of it all marks Russell as one of the arch deceivers of all time.

Repairing the blunders

Down through the years the Society has desperately tried to cover up Russell's prophetic blunders. This cult has always been known for having the best patchwork men in the business. It has been said that this group can take a drop of distilled nonsense and diffuse it into an ocean of verbosity. Among other things they are past-masters in the art of evasion and semantic trickery. It is our candid opinion that the Witnesses are more deserving of the championship belt for exegetical juggling of the scriptures than any other false cult. Yet with all their ingenious ability to twist language, logic, and the scriptures into whatever form they want, the fact remains that they have never been really able to patch up Russell's false prophecies. They have tried! Oh, how they have tried! But the great gaping holes which Russell's false prophecies left in the doctrinal structure of the Watchtower Society were just too much even for their expert patchwork artists to successfully cover up.

In their attempt to repair the damage caused by Russell's false prophecies, the Society even went so far as to put out later editions of Russell's books AND CHANGED THE DATES AND ALSO THE THINGS SAID ABOUT THOSE DATES. This was done to fool the public into believing that these later prophecies were actually Russell's original prophecies! The following evidence will clearly substantiate what we have said here. Dr. B. H. Shadduck, PH.D., in his excellent expose of Russell's prophecies makes this comment:

> "Did Mr. Russell's books tell the date of the (First) World War? They did, after it began. I first heard that

Mr. Russell had foretold the exact date of the outbreak of the war. When I denied this, they gave me 'Studies in the Scriptures' (Russell's books), and there it was, PLAIN ENOUGH TO ASTOUND THE UNWARY. When I compared these books with the earlier edition called 'Millennial Dawn,' the hoax was apparent. In 'Millennial Dawn,' there were very positive statements that all trouble would be over BEFORE 1914" (The Seven Thunders, p. 16).

If more proof is needed, then these next two quotes from Russell's own writings should be enough to convince even the most blind. The quotations which shall be given are not actually "two" but "one." It will be seen that in their first statement they say "before 1914" twice. Yet in their second quote, which is supposed to be an exact duplication of the first, they have changed "before 1914" to read "after 1914." Listen now to what they say in both statements:

"That the deliverance of the saints must take place some time BEFORE 1914 is manifest, since the deliverance of fleshly Israel, as we shall see, is appointed to take place at that time, and the angry nations WILL THEN be authoritatively commanded to be still, and will be made to recognize the power of Jehovah's Anointed. Just how long BEFORE 1914 THE LAST LIVING MEMBERS OF THE BODY OF CHRIST WILL BE GLORIFIED, we are not directly informed; but it certainly will not be until their work in the flesh is done; nor can we reasonably presume that they will long remain after that work is accomplished" (emphasis is ours). Vol. 3, page 228 of Russell's books.

We now produce this same excerpt from the 1923 edition of "Studies in the Scriptures" (Vol. 3, page 228). Notice that in this excerpt "before 1914" has been changed to "after 1914."

"That the deliverance of the saints must take place very soon AFTER 1914 is manifest, since the deliverance of fleshly Israel, as we shall see, is appointed to take place at that time, and the angry nations will then be authoritatively commanded to be still, and will be made to recognize the power of Jehovah's Anointed. Just how long AFTER 1914 the last living members of the body of Christ will be glorified, we are not directly informed; but it certainly will not be until their work in the flesh is done; nor can we reasonably presume that they will long remain after that work is accomplished."

Any false prophet who has ever appeared on the stage of time could easily have exonerated himself if allowed to make such drastic changes in his predictions as BEFORE and AFTER. Let us now briefly examine the material contained in their statement. You will notice that in their first excerpt the glorification of the saints MUST happen BEFORE 1914, because the Jews are supposedly delivered then. Yes, the Jews were certainly delivered — but not BEFORE 1914 as Russell falsely prophesied. They were delivered — six million of them — into Hitler's fiery ovens some thirty years AFTER 1914. Russell certainly proved himself here to be the champion wrong guesser of all time. Russell also tells us in his statement that sometime BEFORE 1914, "the angry nations will then be authoritatively commanded to be still." This certainly turned out to be a colossal lie. The claim of present day brainwashed JW's that their Society prophesied the 1914 World War is shown to be a lie.

The JW's become quite agitated when you begin talking about Russell and his discredited prophecies. The Witnesses will quickly tell you that they are not following Pastor Russell or any other imperfect man. But the fact remains that the Watchtower Society is his brain child. Russell founded the Society and became its first president. This system is all his and has been well named—Russellism. Some JW's will try to justify Russell by saying, "Everyone makes mistakes." The discredited prophecies of Pastor Russell are not just mere mistakes. They are nothing less than false prophecies, and those who make false prophecies ARE FALSE PROPHETS. He that hath ears to hear let him hear: The evidence submitted in these pages conclusively proves that the founder and first president of the Watchtower Society was a liar and a false prophet.

After Russell's death in 1916, Judge Rutherford took over the leadership of the Society and became its second president. Rutherford

ingratiated himself in the eyes of the Society by hi
denouncements of "organized religion" which he term(
You would think that Rutherford would have learned fr
decessor the folly of setting dates. But such was not tl
believed himself to be the mouthpiece of Jehovah for tha
of the startling predictions made by Rutherford is found ii
"Millions Now Living Will Never Die" (dated 1920). Oi
he says —

> "Therefore we may confidently expect that 1925
> mark the return of Abraham, Isaac, Jacob and the fai
> ful prophets of old, particularly those named by t
> Apostle in Hebrews chapter eleven, to the condition
> human perfection."

It would appear there is something drastically wrong he
not one of the old prophets have ever kept any of the appoii
which Russell and Rutherford made for them. The JW's cha
with persecuting them because we dare to mention such thing
why shouldn't we mention them? The Watchtower Society pro(
itself the sole possessor of truth and brands everyone else as (
devil. The evidence clearly shows that the poor souls enmesh(
this system are the victims of a cruel deception. How intelligent n
can be twisted into accepting the wild claims and incredible abs
ities of this cult is difficult to understand. The sheer force of the f
thus far presented should be enough to convince even the most st
born that this system is full of spiritual error and darkness.

Chapter eight

DID CHRIST RETURN IN 1914?

One of the many unscriptural beliefs held by JW's is that the Second Coming of Christ occurred INVISIBLY in 1914. This wild heresy was first spawned in the mind of Pastor Russell who made the following claim:

> "The next chapter will present Bible evidence that 1874 A.D. was the exact date of the 'Times of Restitution', and hence of our Lord's return" (Studies in the Scriptures, Vol. 2, p. 170).

The reader will note there is a time difference of forty years between Russell's belief in the Invisible Second Coming of Christ with that of the present day JW's. The early Russellites firmly believed that Christ came INVISIBLY in 1874. At the end of forty years (1914), this would be verified by many visible events. Well, time rolled on and the visible happenings Russell had prophesied for 1914 failed to take place. Old Father Time had proved Russell to be a false prophet. Many JW's were shaken in their belief and left the Society. Russell died shortly thereafter and Rutherford took control of the floundering ship.

What were they to do now? Rutherford could not claim that all governments were destroyed and no longer in power. He could hardly say that the Millennium had dawned when violence and crime were sweeping the country. So he went to work and juggled things around somewhat until it came out this way. It was during this time that Rutherford was supposed to have had a revelation concerning the Kingdom which Russell had previously prophesied about. The 1914 Kingdom had come all right — but "in the heavens". It was

an invisible Kingdom that could be seen only with the eye of understanding. (How convenient!) The embarrassing parts of Russell's
original prophecy were chipped away. Gone was Russell's claim of
the complete overthrow of all human governments by 1914. Gone
also was the idea of a Paradise Earth for 1914. Thus the prophetic
blunders of Russell were given a whitewash job. The poor dupes in
this system were now given a new revelation to believe. Rutherford
boldly announced to them — "The Kingdom had been established
as the 'new heavens' in 1914 and it must be advertised" (Truth Shall
Make You Free, p. 309).

It seems never to have occurred to the victims of this deception
that since the Society was so very wrong in the past concerning date
setting, then perhaps they are just as wrong today in their setting of
dates. For example, all JW's are now looking forward with great
anticipation to a brand new date which has been given them by the
Society. This new date is 1975! The JW's have been told by the
Society that 1975 will mark 6000 years since Adam's creation.
Wonderful things are expected to take place in 1975! (See Awake
Oct. 8, 1966).

The present day JW's are certainly not showing much respect for
their erstwhile founder, old Pastor Russell. For in his book "The
Time Is At Hand", p. 33, 1907 Ed., Russell claimed that 1872
marked the 6000 years since Adam's creation! It seems as though
these time setting prophets have their chronological calendars mixed
up somewhat. Why can't they get together on this thing? Why must
they always be contradicting themselves?

Christ's second presence

Watch out for this expression: "Christ's Second Presence," for it
is a term used only by JW's. The Witnesses do not believe in the
visible and physical Return of Christ. According to them Christ is
not coming — He is already here! Their claim that Christ's Return
has already taken place is certainly false, because our Lord made
this statement:

"Then if any man shall say unto you, Lo, here is Christ, or there, BELIEVE IT NOT, — For as the lightning cometh out of the east, and shineth even unto the west; so shall also the coming of the Son of man be" (Matt. 24:23, 27).

The Watchtower founder dodged this verse by saying that "lightning" here simply means "bright shining", and that in this text it refers to the gradual dawning of the truth of His Invisible Presence. With this type of exegesis the Bible can be twisted to mean just about anything. Let us pause for a moment and examine Russell's bold attempt to wrest this scripture. You will note that in this text Christ uses the figure of "lightning" to depict His Second Coming. Now all must admit that "lightning" is a *visible thing*. Hence the Return of Christ with His saints will be *visible* even as lightning is visible. If Christ wanted to convey the JW view, namely that His Return would be Invisible, then our Lord would have used an appropriate figure that depicted invisibility such as wind.

Eyes of understanding

The following two texts are absolutely fatal to the Watchtower's false theory that Christ Returned Invisibly in 1914:

"And they shall *see* the Son of Man coming in the clouds of heaven with power and great glory" (Matt. 24:30). Also there is Rev. 1:7 which says, "Behold He cometh with clouds, and every EYE shall SEE Him, and they also which pierced Him; and all kindreds of the earth shall wail because of Him."

These scriptures clearly show that our Lord's Second Coming, His Coming to establish the Kingdom, is therefore a visible one. The JW's make a pathetic attempt to get around these verses by saying, "His return is recognized by the eyes of one's understanding . . ." (Let God Be True, p. 198). This is rich! Have you ever read such exegetical rubbish! They have the nerve to tell us that eyes here mean "the eyes of one's understanding." How utterly absurd! The Bible informs us that "every eye shall see Him" (Rev. 1:7). The Greek word used here for "eye" is the same as is used for "eye" in Matt. 20:34. "So Jesus had compassion on them, and touched their EYES, and immediately their EYES received sight, and they followed Him." Surely this does not mean that it was "their eyes of understanding" that Jesus had given sight to here. Ridiculous! It was their natural eyes that had received sight. Likewise it is with their natural eyes that men shall behold the Coming of Christ in glory to set up His Kingdom. This is but another example of how JW's can put language on the torture rack and stretch all true meaning out of it.

The scriptures thus teach that Christ's Second Coming will be visible and not invisible as the JW's falsely claim. Let us further analyze their save-face interpretation of this text. To begin with, none can argue against the fact that Rev. 1:7 clearly states that at Christ's Return "every eye shall see Him." Now here is the evidence that completely shatters their false teaching of the 1914 Invisible Return of Christ. If Christ came in 1914 as the JW's contend, then everyone living at that time should have seen Christ, either with the literal eye as orthodoxy maintains, or else with "the eye of understanding" as the Watchtower teaches. The question arises, Did everyone living in 1914 see the Return of Christ? We shall let the JW's answer this question for us from their book of doctrine, "Let God Be True," p. 197 which states as follows: "His Witnesses alone saw him leave. Logically only his faithful witnesses would promptly recognize his return." The Witnesses are snared here by the words of their own mouth. For what they say actually destroys their own erroneous interpretation of Rev. 1:7. You will note that the Society states here that only the Witnesses would recognize (see with the eyes of understanding) Christ's Return. Whereas Rev. 1:7 distinctly declares that every eye (literal and otherwise) shall see Christ when He returns. It is clear from this that Christ did not return in 1914, for every eye at that time didn't see Him. Only the Witnesses supposedly saw Him.

The Lord's Supper

The Bible teaches there is a definite time limit to the observance of the Lord's Supper. It is to last only until Christ returns. Hear the words of Saint Paul: "For as often as ye eat this bread, and drink this cup, ye do show the Lord's death TILL HE COME" (1 Cor. 11:26). Now if Christ returned in 1914, then all Christians who celebrate the Lord's Supper today are mistaken! What about the JW's? Certain of their so-called remnant still partake of the Lord's Supper. But how can they scripturally do this if Christ has already returned? This is another hole in their doctrinal structure which they will have difficulty plugging.

The day and hour of Christ's Return

The JW's are always trying to impress others with their so-called knowledge of scriptural things. The Witnesses claim to be the Lord's favourite few because they are the only ones who really know when Christ returned. Let us examine their claim in the light of the following scripture:

> "But of that day and hour knoweth no man, no not the angels of heaven, but my Father only" (Matt. 24:36).

This text clearly shows that no man knows the day and hour of our Lord's Return. The JW's will attempt to save face here by saying, "Oh yes, no man knows the DAY and HOUR of Christ's Return. However, we can know the YEAR of His Return. For notice, all Christ makes mention here of man not knowing is just the day and hour of His Return — nothing whatsoever about the year!"

This is a typical example of how JW's twist and wrest the scriptures unto their own destruction. Surely it is obvious that since man does not know the day and hour of Christ's Return, it is self evident that the year also is unknown. Holy Writ dogmatically informs us that man does not know the day or hour of Christ's Return. The phrase "day and hour" is highly significant, for it strongly suggests that something awesome and cataclysmic will take place ON THE VERY DAY AND HOUR OF OUR LORD'S RETURN. What will happen on the very hour when Christ comes again? When our Lord returns in glory it certainly will not be a secret thing as the JW's teach. The whole world will know about it, for they will see this awesome sight with their own eyes. Listen to what scripture has to say:

> "Immediately after the tribulation of those days shall the sun be darkened and the moon shall not give her light, and the stars shall fall from heaven, and the powers of the heavens shall be shaken. And then shall appear the sign of the Son of Man in heaven, and THEN shall all the tribes of the earth mourn, and they shall see the Son of Man coming in the clouds of heaven with power and great glory" (Matt. 24:29-30).

Did any of these events happen in 1914? Was the sun darkened in 1914? Did the moon refuse to give her light in 1914? Did the stars fall from heaven in 1914? If they did, then where did the stars that are shining right now come from? I suppose that if the Watchtower stated that the present stars in the sky are merely an optical illusion, the JW's would believe it! Did all the tribes of the earth mourn when they saw Jesus in 1914 coming in the clouds of heaven with power and great glory? Notice that it says, ALL OF THE TRIBES OF THE EARTH SHALL MOURN. We know that in 1914 some of the remote tribes of the earth had never even heard of Jesus. How then could these ones mourn about something they knew nothing about? If, on the other hand, there are those who know nothing about Jesus at His Return, but see Him with their literal eyes coming in the sky with power and great glory, they will surely be extremely distressed, even as the scriptures so state.

The personal return of Christ

The Watchtower of Feb. 15, 1955, p. 102 tells us "how" the JW's believe Christ came in 1914.

"Not only are we not to look for Christ to be visible to human eyes, when he comes again, but we should not even think of his leaving heaven and coming within the confines of earth's atmosphere for him to be present. He returns or visits the earth, as did Jehovah in times past, by turning his attention to things of earth."

If Christ's Second Coming consists of nothing more than merely turning His attention to things of earth, our Lord then has returned not twice, but literally millions of times, for is not Christ's attention turned towards this earth every day? Christ gave His followers this promise: "For where two or three are gathered together in my name, there am I in the midst of them" (Matt. 18:20). Hence Christ's invisible presence and attention has always been with His true followers. Our Lord's Return then will be real, Personal and Visible, accompanied with tremendous happenings. Hear what the scripture saith:

"For the Lord Himself shall descend from Heaven with a shout, with the voice of the archangel, and with the trump of God: and the dead in Christ shall rise first. Then we which are alive and remain shall be caught up together with them in the clouds, to meet the Lord in the air: and so shall we ever be with the Lord" (1 Thess. 4:16).

This is what actually transpires when the Lord Returns for His Church. Since this has not happened yet, Christ then certainly did not Return in 1914 as the JW's falsely teach. Our Lord knew that false teachers would deny His Personal Second Coming. This is why He had the Bible Record read, "For the Lord HIMSELF shall descend from heaven with a shout." Note well this word HIMSELF — for it means HE, HIMSELF, PERSONALLY. This is concrete Biblical proof that our Lord will PERSONALLY descend from Heaven at His Second Coming.

The JW's wiggle out from under this condemning evidence by resorting to word trickery. They tell us that the word "return" has a number of meanings. The gist of their argument is "that the word 'return' can mean something else besides a going back bodily to a previous geographical location" (Watchtower, Feb. 1, 1966, p. 70). They thus use this loophole to dodge the Bible teaching of the literal and visible Return of Christ.

The same Watchtower article continues on to show the various senses in which one can "return" without actually returning personally. Listen to their comments:

> "Yet in everyday speech, we often speak of 'returning' in other senses. For example, we say that a person 'has returned to normal health,' or that a deposed ruler has 'returned to power' (although he may never have left his palace)."*

The main weakness in this cunningly devised argument is the fact that the words "health" and "power" are not names of places. THEY ARE ABSTRACT TERMS. When a person returns to health or power, he is returning to a condition and not to an actual place. So when the Bible speaks of the Return of Christ, it is telling us that our Lord shall return — not to some kind of abstract condition — but to an actual place called earth. There is a vast difference between returning to something intangible, such as health and power, and in returning to an actual place.

Their second argument is equally as fallacious as the one we have just answered. The Watchtower further states: "The Bible tells of a number of occasions in which Jehovah 'visited' the nation of Israel. "So his visit was not a literal going to their land but a turning of his attention to them or taking certain action towards them" (Ruth 1:6, Gen. 18:21).

What they say here is quite true. However, there is one noticeable difference between the visitations of Jehovah with Israel and in the Coming of Christ. When God visited Israel He did so as a spirit. Hence in the Old Testament God was invisible to human eyes. But in the New Testament, "the Word was made flesh (visible) and dwelt among us" (John 1:14). When Christ ascended into Heaven the angel announced, "This same Jesus which is taken up from you into Heaven,

* Watchtower, Feb. 1, 1966, p. 70

shall so come in like manner as ye have seen him go into heaven" (Acts 1:11). Notice what the angel says here: "This same Jesus . . . shall so come in like manner." It was a VISIBLE Jesus who ascended into heaven; therefore it will be the SAME VISIBLE Jesus who shall return.

The twisted pattern of their heretical thinking has again been laid bare. With serpentine subtlety they slither through the whole field of Sacred Scripture defiling practically every cardinal truth of the Christian Faith. The crooked path they follow is well marked with the slime of the serpent. It has been shown that their flimsy arguments cannot stand the acid test of scripture. The JW's claim to believe in the Return of Christ. But the facts presented here clearly show that they deny this cardinal truth.

Chapter nine

JUSTIFIED LYING

Not many Christians are aware that JW's are permitted by the Society to lie to you in the interest of their religion. The JW's, of course, do not call this lying! Some of their smart boys at Brooklyn have invented a new name for this kind of deception, they call it practicing "Theocratic War Strategy." The following Watchtower excerpt clearly shows that JW's do indeed lie whenever it suits their purpose:

> "A Witness of Jehovah was going from house to house in Eastern Germany when she met a violent opposer. Knowing at once what to expect she changed her red blouse for a green one in the very next hallway. No sooner had she appeared on the street than a Communist officer asked her if she had seen a woman with a red blouse. No, she replied, and went on her way. Did she tell a lie? No, she did not. She was not a liar. Rather, she was using theocratic war strategy, hiding the truth by action and word for the sake of the ministry" (Watchtower, May 1, 1957, p. 285).

The writer wishes to state at the outset that he does not condemn this poor deceived JW for her lying. She simply did the human thing. She lied to save her own skin. But what we do condemn is the Watchtower's bold attempt to use this incident as an excuse for all JW's to deceive and lie in the interest of their religion. Instead of feeling sorry for one of their own kind, who lied about the fact that she was the JW in the red blouse, the Watchtower congratulates her for acting wisely!

The Watchtower attempts to justify this kind of action by stating that in the Bible Rahab the harlot lied to the King of Jericho in order to protect the Israelite spies. The JW's argue that when Jericho was destroyed, Rahab was spared because she lied to protect the spies. The Bible reveals, however, that Rahab was spared because she acknowledged Israel's God to be the true God (Josh. 2:11). God spared Rahab's life not because she lied, but in spite of the fact that she lied.

The Watchtower further points out that Abraham, Isaac, and David also hid the truth at times. But all this proves is that even the best of men have had their failings. Surely one cannot use the mistakes of any man (no matter how great he may be) as an excuse for wrong doing. The command of the New Testament is clear: "Wherefore putting away lying, SPEAK EVERY MAN TRUTH WITH HIS NEIGHBOUR" (Eph. 4:25). Jehovah's Witnesses, by their own admission, do not speak the truth with their neighbour if it is in their interest not to do so. If they deem it advantageous the JW's will deliberately lie to their neighbour!

The writer has had a number of unpleasant experiences with JW's attempting to palm off this kind of trickery on him. I well remember the day I offered a Witness one of my anti-JW tracts. This JW did not know me personally, but he said that he knew the writer of the tract personally. (He was lying!) Thinking that I was someone else, he began defaming the writer stating that "yours truly" had been booted out of the Watchtower Society in the East for stealing funds from them. (I have never been a JW.) He then sneeringly began denouncing me as an idiot, claiming that I must be really stupid to allow this tract writer to dupe me into handing out his pamphlets. As this JW was venting his spleen against the tract writer and myself (who are one and the same person — only he didn't know it), I showed him my driver's license which proved that I was the tract writer in question. I demanded an apology from this lying JW but got none. The Watchtower gospel had so twisted this man's mind that he couldn't even blush for shame, let alone apologize. This is an example of JW theocratic war strategy — deliberately lying in the interest of their religion.

This JW thought that by lying about the author of the anti-JW tracts that he could discourage Christians from giving them out. Certainly this JW knew that he was lying, but it did not bother him! For had not the Watchtower taught him that it was scriptural for JW's to deceive and lie in the interest of their religion?

The Society claims to be the only voice of truth in the world today. (It is a wonder that the term "truth" does not stick in their throats and choke them.) But how unlike Christ is the Watchtower Society of today. When Peter lied and said that he was not a follower of Christ, did our Lord turn around and smilingly congratulate him ? ? ? Listen to what the scripture has to say: "And the Lord turned, and looked upon Peter. And Peter remembered the word of the Lord, how he had said unto him, Before the cock crow, thou shalt deny me thrice. And Peter went out and wept bitterly" (Luke 22:61-62).

Our Lord certainly does not hand out any bouquets here to Peter; nor does he urge the other disciples to emulate the deceitful actions of Peter in order to protect their person and their cause. What a glaring contrast between what the Bible has to say on this matter compared with what the Watchtower teaches. When our Lord turned and looked at Peter, it was such a look of disappointment that it pierced Peter's very soul. For we are told, "and Peter went out and wept bitterly." A true witness of Jehovah would feel sorry if he weakened under pressure and denied the truth. One can look in vain, but there are no traces of sorrow in the previous quoted Watchtower excerpt concerning the JW woman who deliberately lied to the Communist officer. Where is there any mention of this woman going out and weeping bitterly (as Peter did) because she denied being the JW in the red blouse? It appears that in the eyes of the Society this woman's betrayal of the truth before an opposer served a good purpose. It is well known that the policy of evil and unscrupulous men is that the end justifies the means. Seemingly the JW's have adopted this policy.

One wonders how many Christian martyrs could have been spared if only they had employed the so-called "Theocratic War Strategy" of JW's. With many of them their very lives hung on the answer to this one question. "Are you a Christian?" If they dared to answer "yes," terrible torture awaited them. All they had to do, in many cases, was to deny being a Christian and their lives would be spared.

But these great stalwarts of the Christian Faith stood true to God and proudly confessed that they were followers of Christ. They did not stoop to Watchtower trickery to escape "the tyrant's brandished steel or the lion's gory mane." They lost their earthly lives for the cause of Christ but gained everlasting life and eternal honour. This is our Christian heritage and we have every right to be proud of it.

Chapter ten

THE SOUL

Does man have a soul? According to the JW's the answer to this question is — no! They have gone on record to state, "A human is a soul; he does not possess a soul separate and distinct from the body" (Make Sure Of All Things, p. 349).

This Watchtower heresy is undoubtedly meant to ease the conscience of JW's. For, after all, if man does not possess a soul within him, then the possibility of JW's suffering torment in Hell for their disobedience to God is greatly reduced. This is only wishful thinking on their part, for the Bible clearly teaches that man does have a soul within him, contrary to what the JW's say. Positive proof of this can be clearly seen in Job 14:22 — "his flesh upon him shall have pain, and his soul within him shall mourn." Other scriptures verifying this same truth read as follows: "And the man of God said, let her alone, for her soul is vexed within her" (2 Kings 4:27). The Psalmist cries out: "Why art thou cast down, O my soul? And why art thou disquieted within me?" (Psalm 43:5). We again read, "O my God, my soul is cast down within me" (Psalm 42:6). These scriptures prove beyond any shadow of doubt that man certainly has a soul within him.

The JW's quote Gen. 2:7 in an attempt to prove that man does not possess a soul, but rather is a soul. This text reads: "And God formed man out of the dust of the ground and breathed into his nostrils the breath of life and man became a living soul." See, shouts the JW! Man is a soul; he does not possess a soul. The JW's seemingly have never heard of a figure of speech where a complete object is alluded to by speaking of its principal part. The technical term for such a figure of speech is called synecdoche. Van Baalen commenting on this thought in his Chaos of Cults has well said, "Tell Jehovah's Witnesses that you saw two hundred head of sheep in a pasture, and they will conclude that the heads of sheep had been cut off and thrown on a heap. Inform them that a farmer had twenty hands working for him in the field, and they will at once have a doleful vision of hands floating through space, for man is called a soul in Gen. 2:7, and that means he is all soul."

In 1 Thess. 5:23 we read, "And I pray God your whole spirit and soul and body be preserved blameless unto the coming of our Lord Jesus Christ." This text is irrefutable Biblical evidence that man does possess a soul separate and distinct from the body. Notice the dogmatic Biblical statement here that man consists of three parts — spirit, soul, and body. Without so much as a blush, the JW's will attempt to explain away our proof text in this manner. They will tell you that Paul here is addressing the congregation. Hence when Paul says, "your whole spirit and soul and body be preserved blameless," he is (according to JW's) actually referring, not to individuals, but to the spirit of the congregation, the soul of the congregation (whatever that is), and the body of the congregation!

All the evasive language ever devised by these deceivers will never be able to cover over the plain fact that Paul here is addressing INDIVIDUALS WITHIN THE CONGREGATION. The word "your" denotes personal possession. Paul says, "I pray God YOUR whole spirit and soul and body be preserved blameless." Thus each individual in the congregation possesses a spirit and a soul and a body. Further proof that man possesses a soul separate from the body is found in Psalm 63:1 — "For my soul thirsteth for thee, my flesh longeth for thee in a dry and thirsty land." The reader will note that David here makes a distinction between his soul and his flesh.

The soul at death

Thus far in our study we have shown from the Bible that man definitely possesses a soul which is distinct from his body. We will now show that at death the soul leaves the body and goes either to a place of eternal bliss or to a place of eternal torment. Our first scripture declares, "And it came to pass as her soul was in departing, for she died, that she called his name Benoni" (Gen. 35:18). Coupled with this is the text found at 1 Kings 17:22 — "And the Lord heard the voice of Elijah, and the soul of the dead child came into him again and he revived." These scriptures positively show that at death the soul leaves the body.

The JW's realize only too well that these scriptures prove them wrong. But instead of being humble enough to admit this fact, the Witnesses will still cling with pathetic loyalty to their so-called "God's Only Organization," hoping that the Society can furnish an escape route for them here. These cunning and shrewd schemers will attempt to justify their unscriptural position by twisting the plain meaning of the above proof texts. For example, the JW's teach that when the dead woman's soul departed in Gen. 35:18, it actually means, they say, that it was merely the dead woman's "life" that departed. Also in 1 Kings 17:22, they maintain that it was just "life as a human creature" that returned into the dead boy.

The JW's think that by interpreting the soul in these two texts merely as a principle of life, they will escape the condemning evidence here that brands them as false teachers. The teaching of the Bible is that the soul of man is an intelligent entity. The JW's believe that man's soul is not an intelligent entity but is merely a principle of life. In their zeal to justify their erroneous position, the Witnesses forget that the Bible teaches that "soul" and "life" are not the same. They are distinct one from the other. This truth is revealed in the following text: "He keepeth back his SOUL from the pit, and his LIFE from perishing by the sword" (Job 33:18). It is further written: "Yea his SOUL draweth near unto the grave, and his LIFE to the destroyer" (Job 33:22). We again read, "For my SOUL is full of troubles, and my LIFE draweth nigh unto the grave" (Psalm 88:3). Such scriptures show that God's Word makes a clear distinction between man's soul and his life. This proves therefore that "soul" and "life" are not one and the same thing as the JW's falsely teach.

One JW, with whom we were debating, attempted to dispose of our evidence from Job 33:18 in the following subtle way. He told us that we were wrong to think that "soul" and "life" are distinct from each other just because the Bible lists them separately. You will

102   MASTERS OF DECEPTION

remember that Job 33:18 declares, "He keepeth back his SOUL from the pit, and his LIFE from perishing by the sword." Our JW friend told us that "soul" and "life" in this text is merely a parallel construction — two ways of saying the same thing! (How do you like that for an artful dodge?) Perhaps it should be mentioned that we have previously used this scripture in some of our other writings. It appears that JW leaders have been really digging in order to come up with something that would squash the testimony of this text. They seemingly think that the term "parallel construction" will provide them with an escape route here.

The idea that a parallel construction is two ways of saying the same thing is false. In a book on grammar entitled "English 3200," (p. 485), we are officially given this explanation of a parallel construction: "The principle of expressing similar ideas in a similar or parallel way is known as parallel construction." On page 509 they give us this example of a parallel construction: "The duties of the secretary are to receive visitors, to open the mail, and to type letters." One can see there is a similarity in grammatical construction here, but certainly the three thoughts mentioned in our example are not all one and the same thing. "To receive visitors, to open the mail, and to type letters" does have a parallel construction — BUT EACH ITEM IS DIFFERENT FROM THE OTHER. The same applies in regard to our text: "He keepeth back his SOUL from the pit, and his LIFE from perishing by the sword." We thus have grammatical as well as scriptural proof that SOUL and LIFE are distinct from each other; hence they cannot mean the same thing as JW's falsely teach.

Here are some thoughts on the soul for JW's to consider. If soul means only life as they believe, then in Gen. 2:7 man became a living life! From the Watchtower point of view a dead soul is really a dead life! If soul merely means ANIMAL LIFE, then man became a living animal life! We all know that a tree has life. Does this therefore mean that a tree has a soul? Certainly not!

The soul cannot be killed

The following is perhaps one of the most powerful verses in the whole Bible to prove that the soul of man is eternal. Hearken to this statement coming from our Lord's own lips:

> "Fear not them which kill the body, but are not able
> to kill the soul, but rather fear him which is able to
> destroy both soul and body in hell" (Matt. 10:28).

Regardless of what man might do to the body, he cannot kill the soul. Jehovah's Witnesses can wriggle and wrangle as they may; this is the truth. The soul of man cannot be killed. Scripture proves that the soul of man continues to exist after death, for it is not killed with the body. Once again the Witnesses are proven from the Bible to be false teachers. The devotees of this cult will attempt to get off the hook here by stating the following: "In the Greek Scriptures Matt. 10:28 (N.W.T.)* presents an example where the word 'soul' is used as meaning future life as a soul" (Let God Be True, p. 97). It is obvious that the Society is trying to escape the truth of Matt. 10:28 by confusion of terminology. They would have us believe that the soul Christ is talking about here will not come into existence until the Resurrection! According to the JW's, man can put your present (soulless) body to death but he cannot kill the soul. Why? Because there is no soul in the body to be killed! The soul, you see, (according to JW's) merely means "future life as a soul." And as everyone knows, man at the present moment has only present life — he does not obtain future life until the Resurrection — then (say the JW's) he receives his soul which man cannot kill! What a hodgepodge of ideas! What garbled nonsense! The thought that comes most forcibly to us here is that this cult has more twists than a barrel of pretzels.

The JW's distorted view of soul here is so nonsensical that further comment is unnecessary. Suffice it to say that the soul which is rewarded in Heaven, or punished in Hell, is the same soul that formerly lived on earth. If the ones who receive "future life as a soul" have no soul now (and they don't according to JW's), then it means that God is going to create new future souls at the Resurrection. But how in the name of common sense could these new future souls be justly rewarded for what former non-souls have done! If

---

* JW Bible officially called New World Translation.

ever there were a people lost in a maze of error, it is those who follow
this system.

Destroy in hell

The JW's will try to patch up their shattered theory by quoting the
last part of Matt. 10:28 — "Fear him which is able to destroy both
soul and body in hell." It is certainly true that soul and body can be
destroyed in hell (Gehenna). But destruction in the Bible does not
mean annihilation. These three words — perish, lost, and destroy —
all come from the same Greek term APOLLUMI. According to the
eminent Greek scholar Thayer, APOLLUMI means "render useless,
give over to eternal misery." We read of the wine bottles in Matt.
9:17 that perished: "The bottles break, and the wine runneth out,
and the bottles perish." When the bottle (wine skin) is broken, it
is rendered unfit for its intended use; certainly it has not been
annihilated or reduced to nothing. In Matt. 10:6 we have Christ
sending His disciples to "the lost sheep of the house of Israel." Now
if Apollumi (the Greek word for perish, lost and destroy) means
annihilation — then Christ sent His disciples to the ANNIHILATED
sheep of the house of Israel!

To His people of old Jehovah said, "O Israel thou hast destroyed
thyself, but in Me is thine help, I will be thy king" (Hosea 13:9-10).
This text shows that destruction in the Bible does not mean annihilation or extinction. For how could Jehovah ever be their king if they
were extinct? In Job 19:10 we further read, "He hath destroyed me
on every side and I am gone." Job declares here that he is destroyed
on every side, yet he was still conscious and in existence. We have the
solemn announcement in the Bible concerning those who will
experience "everlasting destruction from the presence of the Lord
and the glory of His power" (2 Thess. 1:9). Everlasting destruction
here does not mean annihilation; it carries the awful thought of being
"given over to eternal misery" (Thayer).

Chapter eleven

SO-CALLED EVIDENCE AGAINST HELL

The Witnesses have several texts which they misapply to back up their contention that Hell is just the grave. Their first scripture reads as follows:

> "For that which befalleth the sons of men befalleth beasts, even one thing befalleth them, as the one dieth so dieth the other, yea they have all one breath, so that a man hath no preeminence above a beast, for all is vanity" (Eccl. 3:19-21).

The JW's argue from this text that there is no difference between man and beast because both die and go to the same place (the grave) and are unconscious. Surely it is obvious that this text is only telling us that as far as death itself is concerned, man certainly is no different from a beast. Because death falls upon both man and beast, "For as one dieth so dieth the other." Nowhere is there any mention here of man being unconscious after death as JW's maintain. Solomon is simply telling us that death brings the bodies of both man and beast down to the same place — the grave. This is clearly announced in these words: "All are of the dust (bodies of both man and beast), and all turn to dust again" (Eccl. 3:20).

In the next verse, Eccl. 3:21, Solomon comments concerning that part of man which lives on after death — the spirit of man, stating that at death the spirit of man goes upward. Solomon again reiterates this truth in Eccl. 12:7. "Then shall the dust return to the earth as it was and the spirit shall return unto God who gave it." From these texts we learn that the spirit of man leaves the body at death. Therefore all of man does not go into the grave as the JW's falsely teach. The

New Testament also proclaims this same truth. You will recall that in Luke 23:46 Jesus says, "Father, into thy hands I commit my spirit." Then again in Acts 7:59 we read where Stephen calls upon God saying, "Lord Jesus, receive my spirit."

The Witnesses well know that these texts just quoted deal a death blow to their false theories. In a vain attempt to justify themselves here they plunge still deeper into their sea of errors and come out all wet, stating that the spirit of man is just his "life force" or "breath." It is quite true that the spirit of man is his "life force," but it is also something much more. In 1 Cor. 2:11 we read, "What man knoweth the things of a man, save the spirit of man which is in him?" Observe here that it is the spirit of man that *knows*. Please note that to the human spirit is attributed human knowledge. We thus have conclusive proof that the spirit of man is an intelligent entity; consequently the spirit of man must be conscious after death seeing it does not go into the grave with the body.

The following scriptures will prove just how wrong JW's are in teaching that the spirit of man is just his "life force" or "breath." In Heb. 12:23 we read about "the spirits of just men made perfect." It would be ridiculous for JW's to say that this text is only referring to "the BREATH of just men made perfect." Likewise it would be equally as ridiculous if they tried to say — "the ACTIVE FORCE of just men made perfect." All can readily see that this text refutes their false theory, for it proves that the spirit of man is a conscious intelligent entity.

To further substantiate this truth we quote Daniel 7:15 — "I Daniel was grieved in my spirit in the midst of my body." It would be absurd for the Witnesses to argue that the spirit of man is just his life force here. Note that this text speaks of Daniel's spirit being grieved. Now in order for Daniel's spirit to feel grief, his spirit would have to possess intelligence. It is an established fact that only intelligent things are able to experience emotion. Hence man's spirit is not just his life force because no kind of force in itself is able to experience grief or any other kind of emotion.

In the following scriptures we will substitute the term "breath" for spirit. This will show the falsity of the JW view that the spirit of man is his breath.

(1) "Jesus perceived in His BREATH that they so reasoned —."
    (Mark 2:8).
(2) "And He sighed deeply in His BREATH —" (Mark 8:12).
(3) "Now while Paul waited for them at Athens, his BREATH was
    stirred in him" (Acts 17:16).
(4) "When Jesus had thus said, He was troubled in BREATH —"
    (John 13:21).
(5) "Let us cleanse ourselves from all filthiness of the flesh and
    BREATH" (2 Cor. 7:1). Does this mean that we have bad breath
    and should use the latest mouth wash?
(6) "The ornament of a meek and quiet BREATH" (1 Peter 3:4).
    Does this mean that we are not to snore?
(7) "Watch and pray that ye enter not into temptation: the BREATH
    is indeed willing, but the flesh is weak" (Matt. 26:41).

The JW's definition of the spirit of man would thus turn the
scriptures into a comedy of errors. How seemingly intelligent minds
can be persuaded to accept such falsehood is difficult to understand.

No wisdom in the grave

> "Whatsoever thy hand findeth to do, do it with all thy
> might, for there is no work, nor device, nor knowledge,
> nor wisdom, in the grave, whither thou goest" (Eccl.)
> 9:10).

This is another text used by JW's to support their position that the
soul is unconscious after death. One will discover in studying the
book of Eccl. that the key phrase is "under the sun." This particular
phrase is found some thirty times in Eccl. The phrase "under the sun"
obviously pertains to things happening in this present life. The
meaning of our text is thus clear. We should make the most of our
earthly opportunities and duties. For when we die and leave this
world all our earthly work, earthly devices, earthly knowledge, and
earthly wisdom will be of no benefit to us in Sheol. This does not
mean that the soul is unconscious in Sheol. Our text is simply telling

us that our earthly occupations will not be possible in Sheol. At death
man enters another realm which is entirely different from our present
world. The soul will enter a new dimension of existence and encounter
new conditions. Hence the former earthly life of the soul will be no
more. This is the reason why there will be no EARTHLY work, or
EARTHLY wisdom, in the grave (Sheol) whither thou goest.

Dead know not anything

> "For the living know that they shall die, but the
> dead know not anything, neither have they anymore a
> reward . . ." (Eccl. 9:5).

This is the main scripture which the JW's use to prove their point
of view. At long last they have found a text which seems to positively
prove that the dead are unconscious. In considering this text please
remember that whatever rule of interpretation you apply to one part
of this scripture, you must also apply to the whole scripture.

If the phrase "the dead know not anything" is to be taken in the
absolute sense (as the JW's maintain), then so must the following
phrase in the same passage be taken in the absolute sense: "Neither
have they (the dead) anymore a reward." Since the JW's have chosen
to interpret this scripture in the absolute sense (because the first phrase
supports their position), then they are forced into denying not only
the resurrection, but also rewards after the resurrection for the
righteous. Since Abraham, Isaac, and Jacob are dead — "neither
have they anymore a reward." Take this scripture in the absolute
sense and it means that all the righteous are cut off from any rewards.
Preposterous! To interpret this text in the absolute sense is to contradict the plain statements of Christ that THE DEAD DO HAVE A REWARD
(Matt. 16:27).

It is obvious there has to be a restriction placed upon Eccl. 9:5 in
order to make it agree with the rest of the Bible. The scripture itself
gives us this qualifying restriction. In Eccl. 9:6 we learn that "the
dead know not anything" . . . UNDER THE SUN. The context thus reveals
that it is only in regard to things now happening "under the sun"

(Eccl. 9:6), that "the dead know not anything" about. Likewise, "neither have they (the dead) anymore a reward" in things now done UNDER THE SUN. The reason the dead are unaware of what is now happening "under the sun" is not because they are unconscious, but rather it is due to the fact that the dead are now in a different realm. Hence their relationship with this present world, which is "under the sun," is cut off.

In 1 Sam. 20:39 we read, "And Jonathan's lad gathered up the arrows, and came to his master. But the lad KNEW NOT ANYTHING." According to the JW's this must mean that the lad was unconscious while running after arrows! In 2 Sam. 15:11 we again read, "And with Absalom went two hundred men out of Jerusalem, that were called, and they went in their simplicity and they KNEW NOT ANYTHING." Will the JW's say that these 200 men were unconscious as they marched along?

These scriptures show us that the phrase "know not anything" has restrictions connected with it. The JW's ignore this fact and by so doing wrest the scriptures unto their own destruction.

No remembrance in Sheol

"For in death there is no remembrance of thee: In the grave (Sheol) who shall give thee thanks?" (Psalm 6:5).

The JW's contend that this scripture teaches cessation of being. However, when examined in its context this passage portrays an entirely different meaning. The whole of the sixth Psalm bears out that David is speaking from the position of a sinner. For remember, David had sinned grievously by taking another man's wife. He was also the cause of this woman's husband being put to death. David finally falls under conviction and realizes that he has indeed sinned and is now only worthy of death. In his anguish David cries out to God for mercy. In the fourth verse David says, "Return, O Lord, deliver my soul, oh save me for thy mercies' sake." Then in the next verse, the one in dispute, Psalm 6:5, David says — "For in death there is no remembrance of thee: In the grave who shall give thee thanks?"

In other words David is saying that if he must die as a sinner without forgiveness, then he will have to go to that part of Sheol where those who are therein do not even remember God; neither do they who are in this place praise God or give Him thanks.

This apparent silence towards God by sinners in Sheol does not prevail because the wicked are unconscious. Rather it is due to the fact that the wicked in Sheol are so full of bitterness and hatred that they have no love for God. Since they have no love for God, why would they ever want to remember Him or give Him thanks?

Thoughts perish

> "His breath goeth forth, he returneth to his earth; in
> that very day his thoughts perish" (Psalm 146:4).

In the Hebrew the word for "thoughts" here is ESTONATH. This word can also mean "purposes" (Young's Concordance). It is thus true that in the very day man dies his thoughts or purposes do perish even as it is written. The reason this happens is not because the dead go into an unconscious state; rather it is due to the fact that death now makes it impossible for the one who has died to carry out the previous thoughts or purposes of his heart. Hence his thoughts perish.

We are told in Luke 12:16 about the rich man who thought within himself to tear down his barns and build bigger ones. But before the rich man could carry out this thought God took his life. Hence when he died this very thought he had within his heart perished or went unfulfilled. This happened not because the rich man became unconscious at death, but because death had now separated him from the land of the living, thereby making it impossible for him to carry out the thoughts he had within his heart.

One wonders if JW's have ever purposed in their heart to do something and then for some reason forgot to do it. Just because their thoughts on the matter perished — DID THEY BECOME UNCONSCIOUS? In Isaiah 55:7 we read these words: "Let the wicked forsake his way, and the unrighteous man HIS THOUGHTS." Does this mean that unrighteous men must quit thinking altogether? Must they become un-conscious and cease to exist because they forsake their thoughts? No! This text refers to purposes. Let the unrighteous man forsake his wicked purposes and God will have mercy on him. It is thus clear from our study that man's "breath goeth forth, he returneth to his earth; in that very day his thoughts (unaccomplished purposes) perish."

The name of the wicked shall rot

"The memory of the just is blessed: but the name of the wicked shall rot" (Prov. 10:7).

The term "name" signifies identity. It is therefore the identity of the wicked that shall rot. You will notice that this is to be a future happening — "shall rot." The question is asked, "When will the name of the wicked rot?" The JW's maintain this happens when the wicked die. But such cannot be the case, for many of the wicked of all ages are still mentioned today in history. Hence the names of the wicked have not yet rotted. The Bible clearly teaches that there is a golden age coming when evil men will be no more. Listen to these blessed words of scripture:

"And God shall wipe away all tears from their eyes; and there shall be no more death, neither sorrow, nor crying, neither shall there be any more pain: for the former things are passed away. And He that sat upon the throne said, Behold, I make all things new" (Rev. 20:4-5).

Just prior to the inauguration of this glorious age, the Bible tells us that the wicked are resurrected and judged according to their works. It is written:

"And I saw the dead, small and great, stand before God and the books were opened: and another book was opened, which is the book of life: and the dead were judged out of those things which were written in the

books, according to their works. And the sea gave up the
dead which were in it; and death and hell (Hades)
delivered up the dead which were in them: and they were
judged every man according to their works. And death
and hell (Hades) were cast into the lake of fire. This is
the second death" (Rev. 20:12-13).

We thus see that the souls of the wicked in Hell (Hades) will be
reunited with their dead bodies that are held in the grip of death.
This is known as the resurrection of the unjust — the coming together of death and Hades. After the wicked are judged according to
their works, they are then cast (both body and soul) into the lake of
fire. This is what the scripture means when it says, "And death and
hell (Hades) were cast into the lake of fire." The Bible calls this
dreadful happening "the second death."

It becomes evident that "the name of the wicked shall rot" when
this awesome event takes place. The reason being that from this point
on God chooses never to remember the wicked any more. Because
God is Almighty, He has the power to forget whatever He wishes to
forget. For example, God has promised to forget the sins of those who
cry unto Him for mercy and pardon. It is written: "I, even I, am He
that blotteth out thy transgressions for mine own sake, AND WILL NOT
REMEMBER THY SINS" (Isa. 43:25).

Still another thing God will forget is the wicked when they are
cast into the lake of fire. This is a fearful thing to contemplate. Just
think of it! God has prepared the lake of fire for the devil and his
angels. But men who die unsaved will also be cast into this dreadful
place (Matt. 25:41). The Lord has set into motion certain fixed
laws that will keep the fires of Hell burning for all eternity. This is
borne out by the fact that Jesus spoke of Hell (Gehenna) as being
a place "where their worm dieth not and the fire is not quenched"
(Mark 9:44). It is a fearsome fact to consider, but Hell is a place
where the fiery worm that never dies will rend and gnaw the miserable
souls of the damned forever.

Those who are damned to the lake of fire will not only be God
forsaken, but they shall also become God forgotten. It is in the final
consummation that "the name of the wicked shall rot." This happens

because God will completely blot them out of His memory. Utterly forsaken and completely forgotten by God and the redeemed, THE WICKED SHALL BE AS THOUGH THEY HAD NOT BEEN (Obadiah 16).

Scripture suggests that just before God blots the wicked out of His memory (as well as the memory of the angels and the redeemed), He allows the righteous to see with their own eyes what they have been saved from. The Bible declares, "Only with thine eyes shalt thou behold and see the reward of the wicked" (Psalm 91:8). This text is fraught with tremendous meaning. The term "reward" here in Hebrew means a *completion*. In other words the righteous of all ages shall behold the END or COMPLETION of the wicked. And according to Christ the completion or reward of the wicked will be — "Depart from Me ye cursed, into everlasting fire, prepared for the devil and his angels" (Matt. 25:41).

Many have wondered why there should be any tears in Heaven. The scriptures indicate that the answer is to be found in this area. When the redeemed are commanded to look into Hell, there to "behold and see the reward of the wicked," such an awful sight will be enough to break every heart. But God has willed that the redeemed see with their own eyes the end result of sin. I believe this will be the saddest moment Heaven shall ever know. It is just after this that "God shall wipe away all tears from their eyes . . . for the former things are passed away" (Rev. 21:4). All memories of unsaved loved ones and friends will be forever erased from the minds of the redeemed. This is when "the name of the wicked shall rot." This is when the wicked "SHALL BE AS THOUGH THEY HAD NOT BEEN" (Obadiah 16). What a solemn thought!

The wicked shall not rise

"O Lord our God, other lords besides thee have had dominion over us: but by thee only will we make mention of thy name. They are dead, they shall not live; they are deceased, they shall not rise: therefore hast thou visited and destroyed them, and made all their memory to perish" (Isaiah 26:16-14).

These "other lords," who for a time had dominion over Israel, were undoubtedly the wicked heathen rulers of Egypt and Babylon. The prophet tells us here that "they are dead, they shall not live." This is not to say they are unconscious. These wicked rulers are dead as far as this world is concerned, for they no longer have physical life. However, even though the wicked are dead they still have existence, but not life. The Apostle John makes this clear when he declares, "He that hath the Son hath life; and he that hath not the Son HATH NOT LIFE" (1 John 5:12). Those who belong to God are the ones who really have life. But the wicked do not have life (eternal life), they merely have existence. This is true not only in our world but also in eternity.

Isaiah then goes on to say, "THEY ARE DECEASED, THEY SHALL NOT RISE." These cruel and wicked lords who oppressed Israel are now dead. They "shall not rise" ever to trouble God's people again. The JW's would have us believe that this phrase — "they shall not rise" — means that the wicked will not be resurrected. Such cannot be true because Christ clearly taught that "all (both righteous and wicked) that are in the graves shall hear his voice. And they shall come forth; they that have done good unto the resurrection of life, and they that have done evil unto the resurrection of damnation" (John 5: 28-29).

Isaiah then continues to say, "Therefore hast thou visited and destroyed them." God did indeed visit Pharaoh and the cruel Egyptian lords with death, for He destroyed them in the Red Sea. Now the JW's will try to tell us that when something is destroyed, it is annihilated. We have already learned that this is not the Biblical meaning of the term "destroyed." Job declared, "He hath destroyed me on every side, and I am gone" (Job 19:10). Everything Job had was marred, or ruined, and broken down. BUT JOB WAS STILL IN EXISTENCE. The wicked, then, when they are destroyed by God are not put out of existence. They are marred, broken down, and brought to a state of ruin. They are given over to a state of eternal misery (Thayer).

We further read where Isaiah declares that God "made all their memory to perish." The words "perish" and "destroy" never signify annihilation in scripture. In 2 Peter 3:6 we read, "The world that then was, being overflowed with water PERISHED." Certainly the world that perished in the flood was not reduced to nothing! When scripture speaks of the wicked as "perishing," or being "destroyed," it is for the purpose of informing us that there is no opportunity for salvation after death for the lost.

In Isaiah 33:14 we are asked, "Who among us shall dwell with everlasting burnings?" Instead of sinners being annihilated, they shall dwell with the everlasting fire. Scripture speaks again and again of the "weeping, wailing, and gnashing of teeth." Those who are consigned to Hell will thus suffer terrible torment. Therefore the wicked are not annihilated. All the grand ideas, thoughts, and purposes which the wicked have in their memory perish at death. This happens not because the wicked are annihilated, but because they cannot fulfill their desires. Hence all the thoughts and purposes which the wicked have in their memory will perish at death because of unfulfillment.

Isaiah certainly regarded Sheol, or the nether regions, to be a place where the dead are conscious. This is evident from his description of the reception given by other souls already in Sheol to the newly arrived soul of the king of Babylon. Describing that reception Isaiah writes: "Hell (Sheol) from beneath is moved for thee to meet thee at thy coming; it stirreth up the dead for thee . . . All they shall speak and say unto thee, art thou also become weak as we? Art thou become like unto us?" (Isaiah 14:9-10). Such conversation in Sheol clearly shows that souls survive the death of the body and are conscious. The Bible tells us of still another conversation in Sheol: "The strong among the mighty shall speak to him out of the midst of hell (Sheol) with them that help him" (Ezek. 32:21). If the dead are unconscious in Sheol — HOW CAN THEY SPEAK OUT?

Dig into hell

"Though they dig into hell, thence shall my hand take them, though they climb up to heaven, thence will I bring them down" (Amos 9:2).

In their book "Let God Be True," (p. 92), the JW's make this comment concerning Amos 9:2. "How can men dig into hell if it is a place of literal fire and sulphur in the bowels of the earth?" The reader will note that Amos 9:2 is not saying that man can dig into hell as the JW's state; neither is God saying that man can climb up to heaven. What God is doing here is posing a hypothetical situation. This is made apparent by the word "though." You will notice that our text says, "THOUGH they dig into hell . . . THOUGH they climb up to heaven." In other words God is saying that even if it were possible for mortal man to go to these extremes (which it is not), His hand could still reach them.

Death

The JW's are fond of quoting Ezek. 18:4 to prove their position: "The soul that sinneth, it shall die." From the Witness point of view, as we have already discussed, death means "extinction, the cessation of being, unconsciousness." This definition of death is utterly false, and not one word in either Greek or Hebrew can be found to uphold their teaching. Death in the Biblical sense is always portrayed as separation. The following will clearly bear this out.

In 1 Tim. 5:6 Paul says, "But she that liveth in pleasure is dead while she liveth." This text shows that a person can be dead (separated from God) but yet conscious. In Eph. 2:1 Paul again states, "You hath he quickened who were dead in trespasses and sins." Before their conversion these Christians were spiritually dead, but yet they were conscious. Also we have the prodigal son's father saying in Luke 15:24 — "For this my son was dead, and is alive again, he was lost and is found." Even though the prodigal son was dead (separated from God), he was still very conscious.

When we come to the text of Ezek. 18:4 — "The soul that sinneth it shall die," the JW's interpret this to mean merely physical death. The context bears out however that the Lord here is talking about another kind of death, namely *the second death*. In Ezek. 18:21 the Lord declares, "If the wicked will turn from all his sins . . . he shall surely live; he shall not die." We know that even the most righteous of men die physically. Hence the Lord here is not talking about physical death. The Lord is saying in this text that if a man will

forsake his sins, follow the commandments, and believe in God —
such a man "SHALL NOT BE HURT OF THE SECOND DEATH" (Rev.
2:11).

Physical death cannot be the full extent of God's wrath against
sinners as JW's teach. This becomes evident by the fact that the
Bible says it is possible for man through repentance "to flee from the
wrath to come" (Luke 3:7). Man cannot flee from physical death,
but he can escape *the terrors of hell* (the second death) by repenting
of his sins and accepting Christ as his Lord and Saviour. If physical
death is the ultimate punishment for sin, then the most ignorant
savage could mete out as great a punishment as Almighty God!

A God of love

The JW's maintain that it is inconsistent to believe that a God of
love could possibly allow any of His creatures to suffer torment in
Hell. Actually this argument has no weight at all, for if God's goodness demands that none of His creatures suffer in eternity, then that
same goodness demands that none of His creatures suffer in this life.
God obviously permits great suffering in this life, and many times we
do not always understand the reason. But one thing is sure — God's
PERMITTING of suffering in this life IS CONSISTENT WITH HIS GOOD-
NESS. Likewise the PERMITTING of suffering in Hell can also be consistent with God's goodness.

Chapter twelve

THE DEAD ARE CONSCIOUS

"And behold there talked with Him two men, which were Moses and Elias, Who appeared in glory and spake of His decease which He should accomplish at Jerusalem" (Luke 9:30).

Here we have the incident of Moses and Elijah, who have been dead for centuries, appearing and carrying on a conversation with Christ. How, then, can the dead be unconscious as the JW's falsely teach? The Witnesses will try to squirm out from under this text by saying that this incident was just a vision and not an actual occurrence! If Moses and Elijah did not actually appear here as the JW's maintain, then with whom was Jesus talking? Was Christ talking to Himself? If what the JW's say is true and Christ was not talking to Moses and Elijah, then why does the Bible tell us here that Christ did speak with them?

The fact that Moses and Elijah appeared and talked with Christ cannot be altered on the grounds that this incident is called a vision in Matt. 17:9. The Bible speaks of those who had seen at the tomb of Christ "a vision of angels" (Luke 24:23). Even the JW's have to admit that the angels seen in this vision were real actual angels. Likewise it was the real Moses and Elijah who appeared and spoke with Christ in this vision.

The dead cry out to God

"I saw under the altar the souls of them that were slain

for the Word of God, and for the testimony which they
held. And they cried with a loud voice saying, How long,
O Lord, holy and true, dost thou not judge and avenge
our blood on them that dwell on the earth" (Rev.
6:9-10).

If the dead are unconscious as the JW's falsely teach, HOW CAN
THEY CRY OUT WITH LOUD VOICES? The JW's will attempt to get
round this text in the following fashion. They will say that this
incident of the martyred souls crying out to God with loud voices
is just the same thing as Abel's blood crying out to God from the
ground (Gen. 4:10). The Witnesses will argue that since Abel's
shed blood was not conscious, consequently neither were these
martyred souls conscious who were crying out to God with loud
voices in Rev. 6:9.

In answering them on this point, it is important to remember that
Abel's shed blood was a sign that murder had been committed. The
following illustration will help make this point clear to us. A good
hunter in the woods will detect certain signs left by animals. These
animal signs speak certain things to an experienced hunter. But certainly they do not speak literal audible language. Likewise the very
presence of Abel's shed blood was a sign that spoke to God. Hence
the two incidents under discussion here are not the same. For in Rev.
6:9 the martyred souls used AUDIBLE WORDS TO CRY UNTO GOD;
whereas in the case of Abel there were no audible words uttered.
Rather it was the SIGN of Abel's shed blood that spoke to God. Therefore the two incidents are not identical.

The witch of Endor

In 1 Sam. 28.3 we read — "Now Samuel was dead and all Israel
lamented him." Yet in 1 Sam. 28:11-16, Samuel returns from the
dead and pronounces Saul's death sentence. The JW's realize that
this account in scripture poses a problem for them. Therefore they
will attempt to explain it away by stating that it was not actually the
real Samuel who came back from the dead, but rather it was only
a demon impersonating him.

The Bible, however, tells us a different story. Scripture declares that when the witch saw Samuel she "cried with a loud voice" (1 Sam. 28:12). Now if Samuel was not the real Samuel here but only a demon impersonating him — WHY WOULD THE WITCH CRY OUT? It is quite obvious that the reason the witch became frightened was because the real Samuel had appeared instead of her familiar spirit. In other words God had overruled and allowed the real Samuel to appear to pronounce judgment upon Saul. Then in 1 Sam. 28:19 we have Samuel saying to Saul — "Tomorrow shalt thou and thy sons be with me." The following day Saul and his sons went into battle, they were slain, their bodies were taken and nailed to the walls of Bethshan, and some two or three days later their dead bodies were taken down and burned. This certainly shows that Saul and his sons were not in the grave with Samuel the day they died. Then where were they? Saul and his sons at death went to Sheol or Hades — the realm of the spirit world.

Let us not forget the fact that it is the Holy Spirit who is giving us this record. In 1 Sam. 28:12 the Holy Spirit says, "And when the woman saw Samuel . . ." According to the Holy Spirit the witch actually saw the dead Samuel, not a demon impersonating him. This remarkable incident has been recorded for us by the Holy Spirit. And when the JW's try to explain away the actual appearance of Samuel here (because this incident contradicts their teaching), they are trifling with the eternal Word of God.

The inner man

> "For which cause we faint not; but though our OUT-
> WARD MAN perish, yet the INWARD MAN is renewed day
> by day. While we look not at the things which are seen,
> but at the things which are not seen: for the things which
> are seen are temporal, but the things which are not seen
> are eternal" (2 Cor. 4:18).

The Apostle Paul informs us here that the outward (or physical) man will eventually perish. He then tells us that "the inward man is renewed day by day." This part of man which Paul calls "the inward man" (or soul) does not perish with the body. Hence the INWARD MAN, which is the soul of man, IS ETERNAL. Paul further tells us in this text that "the things which are seen are temporal; but the things which are not seen are eternal." We all know that the physical body of man can be seen; therefore it is temporal and will perish. But there is a part of man which Paul calls here "the inward man" (or soul) that is unseen, and which is eternal.

Heart lives forever

"The meek shall eat and be satisfied: they shall praise the Lord that seek him: YOUR HEART SHALL LIVE FOR-EVER" (Psalm 22:26).

The Psalmist tells us here that man's "heart shall live forever." In Holy Scripture the heart means that part of man with which he thinks and believes. The following scriptures will substantiate this fact. "For as he (man) thinketh in his heart, so is he" (Prov. 23:7). "With the heart man BELIEVETH unto righteousness" (Rom. 10:10). "Lest they should UNDERSTAND with their heart . . ." (Matt. 13:15).

The heart of man is therefore the KNOWING part of man, or the seat of man's intelligence. And it is this part of man, the heart of man, THAT LIVETH FOREVER; hence man's true self, his soul, is eternal.

Death cannot separate us from God's love

"For I am persuaded that neither DEATH, nor life, nor angels, nor principalities, nor powers, nor things present, nor things to come, nor height, nor depth, nor any other creature, shall be able to separate us from the love of God, which is in Christ Jesus our Lord" (Rom. 8:38-39).

Since death cannot separate us from the love of God, consequently there must be a part of man that exists after we die. In the preceding proof we established that the conscious part of man is his heart. You will recall that our scripture said, "Your heart shall live forever." When the love of God is in our hearts, we are conscious of it. Therefore death cannot destroy our consciousness of God's love. This clearly shows that the dead cannot be unconscious as the Witnesses maintain.

The statement is made in Holy Writ that "Love never faileth" (1 Cor. 13:8) The term "love" means strong feeling or affection. Love is a quality of the soul. Since the Bible teaches that love is to continue, THEN THE PART OF MAN WHICH LOVES WILL ALSO CONTINUE TO EXIST AFTER DEATH. And since it is the HEART or SOUL of man which loves, it is therefore this part of man that is eternal.

A Christian never dies

"And whosoever liveth and believeth in Me shall never die" (John 11:26).

Christ clearly teaches in this passage that a faithful Christian will always have conscious, unending existence with God. Certainly our text cannot be referring to physical life here on earth. This becomes self evident when we consider Heb. 9:27 — "It is appointed unto man once to die and after this the judgment." The part of man that never dies is called in scripture "the inward man" (2 Cor. 4:16), "your heart that lives forever" (Psalm 22:26). Jesus said the same thing in these words: "And fear not them which kill the body, BUT ARE NOT ABLE TO KILL THE SOUL" (Matt. 10:28).

Blessed are the dead

"Blessed are the dead which die in the Lord from henceforth" (Rev. 14:13).

The Greek scholar Thayer defines the term "blessed" here as meaning "blessed or happy." The JW's maintain that the dead are unconscious, but this text informs us that those who die in the Lord

are happy. In what way could an unconscious man be happy? The
fact that the righteous dead are blessed, or happy, is positive proof
that departed Christians are conscious. From the JW point of view our
text merely means — "Blessed are the UNCONSCIOUS DEAD which die
in the Lord." How absurd! We are told in Psalm 116:15, "Precious
in the sight of the Lord is the death of his saints." Surely this suggests
that those who die in the Lord remain conscious and are in a happy
state. However if we apply the JW definition of death to this passage
it becomes ludicrous: "Precious in the sight of the Lord is the UN-
CONSCIOUS STATE of his saints."

Present with the Lord

> "We are confident, I say, and willing rather to be absent
> from the body, and to be present with the Lord" (2 Cor.
> 5:8).

Who is the "WE" in this text? The pronoun "WE" in this passage
obviously refers to the spirit, or soul, which resides within the body.
If Paul went into a state of unconsciousness at death, how could he
possibly be present with the Lord while absent from the body? Paul
further states in Phil. 1:21, "For to me to live is Christ, AND TO DIE
IS GAIN . . . For I am in a strait betwixt the two, having a desire to
depart and be with Christ which is far better." If the JW's are right
and death means unconsciousness, how could Paul have gained by
going into a state of unconsciousness? How could it be far better for
Paul to be with Christ IF HE WERE UNCONSCIOUS?

Another text tells us, "'For to this end Christ both died, and rose,
and revived, that He might be Lord both of the dead and living"
(Rom. 14:9). The scripture announces here that Christ rose to be
Lord of the dead and the living. According to the JW's the dead pass
into a state of nothingness. Therefore this can only mean that Christ
rose from the dead that He might be the Lord of the NOTHING and
the living. The whole JW doctrinal structure is riddled with such
absurdities.

Chapter thirteen

THE DOCTRINE OF HELL TORMENT

"The rich man also died and was buried; And in hell
he lift up his eyes being in torments" (Luke 16:23).

This solemn portion of scripture, which was uttered by Christ
Himself, is a real sore thorn in the sides of JW's. The blinding power
of Watchtower prejudice will not allow them to accept this scripture
as it actually reads. The devotees of this cult have been brainwashed
into believing that this scripture does not really mean THERE IS
TORMENT IN HELL. The JW's will quickly tell you that the doctrine
of hell torment is the devil's lie. From the JW point of view it appears
that Christ is guilty of preaching the devil's doctrine! What utter
nonsense! The doctrine of "hell torment" is the teaching of Christ.
Our Saviour clearly taught this terrible truth and we would do well
to heed His many warnings concerning the awfulness of Hell. If the
doctrine of Hell torment is Satan's lie as the JW's maintain, then
Christ stooped to using a devil's lie in order to illustrate a spiritual
truth! Certainly Christ would never attempt to teach truth from an
illustration that contained lies.

In their attempt to escape the condemning evidence of this text,
the JW's will say that Christ was not speaking the literal truth when
He said — "The rich man also died and was buried; and in Hell he
lift up his eyes being in torments." According to the JW's Christ was
only giving a parable here. The account of the rich man and Lazarus
is certainly not a parable but a true happening, borne out by the fact
that Christ declared: "There *was* a certain rich man . . ." This certain
rich man actually did live, and he died, and after death he went to
Hell AND WAS IN TORMENTS. If this did not really happen, then Christ
is guilty of telling an untruth.

Those who say that the account of the rich man in Hell is not an actual happening are accusing Christ of leaving Himself open to be misunderstood. Christ would not tell us there was TORMENT IN HELL if such a thing didn't exist. Also the personal names of Abraham and Moses, which are mentioned in this account, are further proof that this incident is not a parable. The clinching evidence which proves beyond all doubt the reality of the rich man being tormented in Hell is found in the following scripture:

> "But without a parable spake He not unto them (the multitude): and when they were alone, He expounded all things to His disciples" (Mark 4:34).

If the account of the rich man in Hell is a parable as the JW's insist, then we challenge them to show us where Christ ever expounded the meaning of this so-called parable to His disciples! The Witnesses will have to admit that Christ never did explain the parabolic meaning of the rich man being tormented in Hell. This in itself is positive proof that Christ meant this incident to be taken as an actual fact and not as a parable. If this were a parable, THEN CHRIST WOULD HAVE EXPOUNDED THE MEANING OF IT TO HIS DISCIPLES (Mark 4:34). Since Christ didn't do this, then unquestionably He meant His words here to be understood exactly as they were uttered.

What would be the purpose of Christ telling a parable here if it had no significance? And if this so-called parable did have some significance, then why doesn't the Bible tell us what it is? The theory that the account of the rich man being tormented in Hell is merely a parable has some glaring weaknesses indeed.

Some will try to say that the point we have just raised here is not valid because of the fact that Christ gave other parables and yet did not explain them. It is true that on occasion our Lord did speak parables to the people without explaining them. But the reason He did this is given in the following scripture:

> "And the disciples came and said unto Him, Why speakest thou unto them in parables? He answered and said unto them, Because it is given unto you to know the mysteries of the kingdom of heaven, but to them it is not given" (Matt. 13:10-11).

We gather from what is said in this portion of scripture that Christ did not always explain the meaning of His parables to the people. But such was not the case with our Lord's disciples. The Bible plainly tells us here that Christ said unto His disciples: "Because it is given unto you TO KNOW the mysteries of the kingdom of heaven, BUT TO THEM IT IS NOT." This agrees perfectly with Mark 4:34. "He expounded all things to his disciples." It is clear from this that Christ must have explained the meaning of His parables to the disciples. But in the case of the rich man suffering torment in Hell, no meaning or explanation of this so-called parable is given to the disciples. This forces us to conclude that Christ was relating a factual account when He declared: "The rich man also died, and was buried; And in Hell he lift up his eyes being in torments" (Luke 16:22-23).

Perhaps the reader would be interested in knowing how the JW's interpret this portion of scripture. Brace yourself for a sickening jolt. Here it is:

> "The rich man represents the ultraselfish class of the clergy of Christendom, who are now afar off from God and dead to his favour and service and tormented by the Kingdom truth proclaimed. Lazarus depicts the faithful remnant of the body of Christ. These, on being delivered from modern Babylon since 1919, receive God's favour, pictured by the 'bosom position of Abraham,' and are comforted through His Word" (Let God Be True, p. 98).

Well, there you have it! With this type of exegesis the Bible can be twisted to teach anything and everything. Their heretical position has again forced them to come on stage and perform another scripture juggling act. Surely such wild interpretation of God's Word is enough to strain credulity to a bursting point. This is a prime example of their bold and reckless misuse of scripture. It appears that JW's will go to any lengths in order to escape the blast of any scripture that brands them for what they really are — FALSE TEACHERS.

Parable of the tares

One portion of scripture that completely disarms the JW deceivers, leaving them speechless, is Christ's interpretation of the parable of the tares. You will recall that Christ said in this parable, "Gather ye together first the tares, and bind them in bundles to burn them" (Matt. 13:30). What does this mean? Dropping down to Matt. 13:38, Christ explains that "THE TARES ARE THE CHILDREN OF THE WICKED ONE." Our Saviour then tells us what is going to happen to these wicked ones. "As therefore the tares are gathered and burned in the fire; so shall it be in the end of the world" (Matt. 13:40). Christ then announces that He will take the tares (the wicked), "AND SHALL CAST THEM INTO A FURNACE OF FIRE; THERE SHALL BE WAILING AND GNASHING OF TEETH" (Matt. 13:42).

This portion of scripture is given in such a manner that any attempt to explain it away is useless. Since this scripture is Christ's own explanation of the parable of the tares, IT THEREFORE HAS TO BE TAKEN JUST AS IT READS. Hence any attempt on the part of JW's to explain away Christ's explanation here proves futile indeed. This scripture thus proves conclusively that Christ certainly did teach the doctrine of hell torment.

> "Error now wounded writhes in pain
> and dies among his worshippers."

There is indeed a dreadful place called Hell awaiting those who die without Christ. The Bible declares, "It is a fearful thing to fall into the hands of the living God" (Heb. 10:31). Hell is the place where God will vindicate His outraged majesty. Jesus tells us that the wicked shall be consigned to the lake of fire with the pronouncement of these terrible words: "DEPART FROM ME, YE CURSED, INTO EVERLASTING FIRE PREPARED FOR THE DEVIL AND HIS ANGELS" (Matt. 25:41). Hell is a place where lost souls are forever weeping and wailing and gnashing their teeth in the hopelessness of remorse and mad despair. This is where the damned shall drink the wine of the wrath of God. This is where "the smoke of their torment ascendeth up forever and ever" (Rev. 14:11). This is that dreadful place where all the fury and terror of Almighty God is unleashed. Sinners in the hands of an angry God. Oh the thought of it! Paul said, "Knowing therefore the terror of the Lord, we persuade men" (2 Cor. 5:11).

Why devils tremble

"Thou believest that there is one God; thou doest well,
the devils also believe AND TREMBLE" (James 2:19).

Why do the demons tremble? The reason demons tremble is because
they know there is a place of "EVERLASTING FIRE PREPARED FOR THE
DEVIL AND HIS ANGELS" (Matt. 25:41). This is why the demons said
to Jesus, "Art thou come hither TO TORMENT US before the time?"
(Matt. 8:29). The demons certainly know there is a time coming
when they will be tormented in everlasting fire.

Sorer punishment

"He that despised Moses' law died without mercy under
two or three witnesses: Of how much SORER PUNISH-
MENT, suppose ye, shall he be thought worthy, who
hath trodden under foot the Son of God . . ." (Heb.
10:28-29).

There is A WORSE PUNISHMENT awaiting sinners who do "despite
unto the spirit of grace" than for the wicked who were put to death
without mercy under the law of Moses. If annihilation is God's punishment for the wicked (as the JW's affirm), then how can there
possibly be this greater or worse punishment for those who trample
Christ under their feet? The theory that the wicked are annihilated
breaks down here, for annihilation would give all the wicked the
same punishment, and hence would make it impossible for this added
degree of "worse punishment" to exist.

The Divine decree of "worse punishment" will be meted out in a
Hell composed of different planes, each plane in Hell more terrible
than the other. King David declared, "Thou hast delivered my soul
from the lowest hell" (Psalm 86:13). Since the JW's believe that Hell
is merely the grave, perhaps they can answer this question. Just how
far down in the earth is this "lowest Hell" (or grave)?

The JW's do not believe that Hell is a place of torment; they maintain that Hell is simply the grave. What does the Bible say? "The wicked shall be turned into hell (Sheol) and all the nations that forget God" (Psalm 9:17). If Hell is merely the grave, then why does the Bible state here that it is just the wicked who go there? Surely the righteous also go to the grave! The Hell spoken of here cannot be the grave because the righteous are exempt from going there.

Hell is not the grave

"Withhold not correction from the child: for if thou beatest him with the rod, he shall not die. Thou shalt beat him with the rod, and shalt deliver his soul from hell (Sheol)" (Prov. 23:13-14).

If Hell is merely the grave, then this text teaches that by using the rod of correction you can deliver a child's soul *from the grave!* We know this is not true; for the righteous and wicked both go to the grave. This text actually conveys the thought that if you bring up a child properly, using adequate correction when necessary, doubtless you will be instrumental in delivering his soul from going to Hell.

Everlasting fire

"And if thy hand offend thee, cut it off: it is better for thee to enter into life maimed, than having two hands to go into hell, INTO THE FIRE THAT NEVER SHALL BE QUENCHED. Where their worm dieth not, and the fire is not quenched" (Mark 9:43-44).

This fearsome statement was spoken by Christ. Our Saviour speaks here of a fire THAT NEVER SHALL BE QUENCHED. The JW's believe that whenever Christ spoke about Hell fire, He did so only in a figurative sense. To a JW Gehenna simply means the smoldering fires in the valley of Hinnon. This particular valley was situated outside

Jerusalem, and the Jews of Christ's day burnt their garbage along with the dead bodies of criminals in this place. But surely Christ was not referring to the fires of a garbage dump when He spoke of ever-lasting fire (Matt. 25:41). No! For today the fires in the valley of Hinnon ARE NOT BURNING. Hence the fire Christ is talking about is an entirely different kind of fire. It is an everlasting fire AND SHALL NEVER BE QUENCHED.

Notice that in our text Christ makes this solemn announcement: "Their worm dieth not and the fire is never quenched." The word "their" denotes possession. Obviously something that belongs to a lost soul in Hell never dies. Jesus declared that the part of man that never dies in Hell is "their worm." Some Christian scholars maintain that the worm which never dies in Hell is the gnawing conscience of the lost. Whatever it may be, this one fact is undeniable — JESUS DECLARED THERE IS SOMETHING IN HELL THAT NEVER DIES. Hence Hell cannot be a place of total annihilation as the JW's falsely teach. Since Hell fire is everlasting, one can only conclude that the lost must everlastingly be in existence to endure the unquenchable fires of Hell. If the wicked are merely annihilated, then why the need for Hell fire to be *everlasting?*

Tormented forever and ever

Words to a JW do not mean what ordinary people understand them to mean. The JW's have a vocabulary all their own. They have redefined and given an entirely new meaning to words in the Bible which contradict what they believe. This is the kind of evasive tactics one has to cope with when dealing with these people. One prime example where they redefine the meaning of Bible words, because such words clearly contradict their "no torment in Hell heresy," is Rev. 20:10.

> "And the devil that deceived them was cast into the lake of fire and brimstone, where the beast and false prophet are, AND SHALL BE TORMENTED DAY AND NIGHT FOREVER AND EVER."

The word "tormented" here has a very restricted meaning. It comes from the Greek word BASANIZO and literally means "TO TORTURE," or "TO VEX WITH GRIEVOUS PAINS" (Thayer's Greek Lexicon p. 96). The devil then will be tormented (vexed with grievous pains) forever in the lake of fire. This fearsome text deals a fatal blow to their "no torment in Hell heresy." In an attempt to escape the scorching rebuke of this scripture, the JW's simply pull their redefinition switch and PRESTO! The term "tormented" here no longer means "to vex with grievous pains," but instead comes out of the JW word-changing computer meaning MERE ANNIHILATION OR EXTINCTION!

The sting from this scripture forces them to cry out: "This scripture does not mean what it says because it is symbolical." This term SYMBOLICAL is quite an escape hatch for these trick artists. They seem to think the word SYMBOLICAL is some kind of a magical wand. The JW's believe that all they have to say is SYMBOLICAL and presto! All texts that literally contradict their Watchtower heresies, lo and behold, no longer do so! Such is the depth of their delusion.

How can Rev. 20:10 be symbolical when the Witnesses admit that the devil is not symbolical BUT REAL! The startled JW's will reply, "The devil is real, but the lake of fire which he is cast into and the torment he suffers is symbolical." The JW concept of this text is an absurd farce, for it compels them to accept the ridiculous conclusion that God is going to cast a real devil into a symbolical lake of fire THAT DOES NOT ACTUALLY EXIST! The courts of our land do not send a criminal to a symbolical prison, but to a real prison. Satan, the greatest of all criminals, will be cast into God's real prison. It is called the lake of fire.

The Witnesses maintain that the devil is going to be put out of existence. How can this be true when the Bible plainly states that the devil "SHALL BE TORMENTED DAY AND NIGHT FOREVER AND EVER." It is a contradiction in terms to believe that a non-existing entity can be tormented. How can the devil suffer torment forever AND YET NOT FEEL THIS TORMENT? The twisted logic of Watchtower representatives defies all reason and is indeed a head shaking wonderment.

Chapter fourteen

ANOTHER GOSPEL

The JW's erroneously teach that only 144,000 will ever go to Heaven. In the early days of this cult such a teaching really posed no problem for them. However, as time rolled on the number of JW's began to exceed the set quota of 144,000. What were the leaders of this cult to do now? Necessity became the mother of invention. It was obvious that the overflow crowd would not stay if there was nothing for them. Thus it was that Rutherford announced in 1931 that the door to Heaven was now closed. But the overflow crowd (the other sheep) were told not to despair because Jehovah's mouthpiece, Rutherford, had been given a new revelation! The destiny of the overflow crowd, called the other sheep, was to be LIFE EVERLASTING HERE ON EARTH. All of this chaos and confusion finally resulted in JW's dividing themselves into two distinct classes by 1935. One group became the heavenly class of 144,000; the other was called "the earthly class." The latter was destined to grow into an innumerable number. The majority of present day Witnesses claim to belong to the earthly class. This is why JW's of today will tell you that they have no desire to go to Heaven, for their hope is to live here forever on earth. These JW's maintain that since Heaven is not to be their home, THEY DO NOT NEED TO BE BORN AGAIN!

Before we continue, let us make a few comments on what has been said thus far. The Society claims that the door to Heaven is now shut. Perhaps we should mention there are some 9000 living JW's who lay claim to being part of the 144,000. These are the only ones left in our present world who will supposedly ever go to Heaven. Yet there is always a chance that one of these favoured 9000 will fall away from the truth (leave the JW's). If this should happen then a sign will

immediately be posted reading: "VACANCY IN HEAVEN (for one)."
How the Witnesses go about filling up these odd vacancies in Heaven
when they come up is not quite clear. Presumably it is on a seniority
basis.

We challenge JW's to prove from scripture that the door to Heaven
is now shut for mankind. Our Saviour opened the door to Heaven
for man by His death, resurrection and ascension. Christ declares,
"I have set before thee an open door AND NO MAN CAN SHUT IT"
(Rev. 3:8). How dare these false prophets claim that the door to
Heaven is now shut for mankind. Jesus is the One "that openeth AND
NO MAN SHUTTETH" (Rev. 3:7). The door to Heaven has been opened
wide for all those who will accept Christ as their Lord and Saviour.
One cannot help but recall the stinging rebuke Christ hurled at the
religious hypocrites of His day: "Woe unto you, scribes and Pharisees,
hypocrites! FOR YOU SHUT UP THE KINGDOM OF HEAVEN AGAINST
MEN" (Matt. 23:13). The Watchtower Society is guilty of what Christ
denounced the scribes and Pharisees for doing — SHUTTING UP THE
KINGDOM OF HEAVEN AGAINST MEN.

The 144,000

The JW's quote Rev. 7:4 and also Rev. 14:1-3 to show that only
144,000 will ever go to Heaven. One can search in vain, but nowhere
does the Bible say that the 144,000 are the only ones among mankind
who will ever go to Heaven. This is mere conjecture on the part
of JW's.

The very most JW's can show us is that the 144,000 were given
the honour of singing a new song which others could not sing (Rev.
14:3). This honour seems to be due to the fact that they are a special
class of REDEEMED MEN. Holy writ tells us concerning the 144,000:
"These are they which were not defiled with women, for they are
virgins" (Rev. 14:4). Since the JW's interpret the magical number
144,000 as being literal, consequently, to be consistent, they should
also interpret what is said about the 144,000 as being literal. If the
Witnesses were consistent in their interpretation here, they would
have to believe that women are exempt from the 144,000 class. Hence

if the 144,000 are the only ones going to Heaven as JW's teach, then this can only mean there will be no women in Heaven!

The Witnesses should note that the 144,000 are said to be Jews, not Gentiles. The JW argument that they are "spiritual Israel" is not valid because the 144,000 ARE ALL NAMED BY TRIBE. The Bible plainly states that there were sealed twelve thousand out of each of the twelve tribes of Israel. The Bible then goes on to specifically list the twelve tribes by name (Rev. 7:4-8). This shows that the 144,000 are redeemed Jews.

The earthly class

"After this I beheld, and, lo, a great multitude, which no man could number, of all nations, and kindreds, and people, and tongues, stood before the throne, and before the Lamb, clothed with white robes, and palms in their hands" (Rev. 7:9).

The Watchtower teaches that the earthly class of JW's is clearly depicted here in Rev. 7:9. One can read and re-read this text, but nowhere does it say that this "great multitude" are exempt from Heaven. Neither does it say they are relegated to live here on earth. In actual fact the term "earth" isn't even mentioned in connection with the great multitude.

The Bible states that the great multitude, "which no man could number" (the so-called JW earthly class) — "stood BEFORE THE THRONE and before the Lamb" (Rev. 7:9). According to the Bible this "great multitude" class are in Heaven because they "STOOD BEFORE THE THRONE." The JW's will reply, "This doesn't prove anything at all because those on the earth also STAND BEFORE GOD'S THRONE." Their vain attempt to evade the clear meaning of our text is fruitless because of the fact that the angels are also said to be "BEFORE THE THRONE" (Rev. 7:11). Even the 144,000 are "BEFORE THE THRONE" (Rev. 14:3). We thus see that the angels, the 144,000, and the great multitude are in Heaven, for they are all BEFORE THE THRONE.

We are further told concerning the "great multitude": "Therefore are they before the throne of God, and serve Him day and night IN HIS TEMPLE" (Rev. 7:15). Scripture tells us that God's temple is in Heaven. Here is the proof for this statement: "And the *temple of God* was opened in Heaven" (Rev. 11:19). Again we read, "And another angel came out of *the temple* which is in Heaven" (Rev. 14:17). What further proof is needed? The "great multitude" cannot be an earthly class as JW's falsely teach because they serve God day and night in His temple WHICH IS IN HEAVEN. This is conclusive proof that the "great multitude" are part of the redeemed in Heaven.

In concluding our thoughts on the "great multitude" theme we quote one more scripture: "They shall hunger no more, neither thirst any more, NEITHER SHALL THE SUN LIGHT ON THEM, nor any heat" (Rev. 7:16). The destiny of the "great multitude" then cannot be the earth, for we are distinctly told here "neither shall the sun light on them."

The Bible gives us this wonderful description of Heaven: "And there shall be no night there; and they need no candle, NEITHER LIGHT OF THE SUN, for the Lord God giveth them light: and they shall reign forever and ever" (Rev. 22:5). We thus see that the "great multitude" will be in Heaven because the sun shall not light on them, for the Lord God will be their light.

The other sheep

The JW's often refer to the "great multitude" as the "other sheep." They get this in John 10:16. "And other sheep I have, which are not of this fold: them also I must bring, and they shall hear my voice; and there shall be *one fold* and one shepherd." The JW's will say that the "other sheep" mentioned here by Christ are actually the present day earthly class of JW's. They have surely stretched this one! If what they say here is true, then this statement uttered by Christ held no relevance for His immediate hearers. Thus the JW point of view logically leads to the senseless conclusion that the term "other sheep" held no meaning for the people of Christ's day. We are supposed to believe that it took some 1900 years for this term "other sheep" to take on meaning. The very fact that Christ said, "and other sheep I HAVE" shows that he had these "other sheep" at the time He made this statement. The phrase, "I have" denotes present possession. Then who were these "other sheep" Christ had when He spoke these words? The answer to this question is twofold. First, there were the Old Testament saints, called prisoners of hope (Isa. 14:17), who waited in the Paradise section of Hades for Christ to come and take them home to Heaven. All God fearing Gentiles would likewise be Christ's "other sheep."

If Christ wanted to convey the JW view, namely that the "other sheep" would not be in existence for some 1900 years, then He would have spoken IN THE FUTURE TENSE: "And other sheep I (will) have." But our Saviour does not speak here in the future tense, He speaks in the present tense. This shows that the JW's are wrong in teaching that Christ was referring to some 1900 years in the future when He spoke about the "other sheep."

Please notice that in this text Jesus declares — "There shall be ONE FOLD (literally one flock), and one shepherd" (John 10:16). This scripture certainly knocks the props from under the JW theory that the redeemed of the Lord are divided into TWO distinct separate classes, one group supposedly the earthly class and the other a heavenly class. Jesus plainly tells us here: "THERE SHALL BE ONE FOLD." In the light of this scripture, why do the JW's teach that the Lord's sheep are divided into an earthly and heavenly class? It is clear from what Christ said that in the final consummation all of the Lord's sheep will become ONE FLOCK and Christ shall be their shepherd.

Old Testament saints

The JW's have also barred all the Old Testament prophets from going to Heaven. They have to do this in order to make their theory fit that only 144,001 will go to Heaven. (The one other is Christ Jesus.) These faithful worthies of old have all been ordered by the Witnesses to come and live with them on the New Earth. If the JW's were wise they would heed this word of caution. They should immediately send some kind of an S O S to Elijah cancelling their previous order that he come and join them on the New Earth. For if Elijah ever did come among them some heads would certainly roll. Obviously this would have to be the case, for didn't Elijah order the false prophets of his day to be taken and slain?

The Old Testament prophets will most certainly be in Heaven because Jesus said: "Many shall come and shall sit down with Abraham, and Isaac, and Jacob IN THE KINGDOM OF HEAVEN" (Matt. 8:11). One JW Congregational Servant tried to explain away this text in the following manner. With impudent arrogance he told us that this text was not actually talking about the real literal Abraham, Isaac and Jacob being in the Kingdom of Heaven. Oh, no! We were told that Christ here is speaking figuratively. Abraham, you see, is supposed to represent Jehovah God, Isaac represents Christ Jesus, and Jacob represents the 144,000 ! ! ! Our reply to this kind of wholesale butchery of the Bible was Luke 13:28 — "There shall be weeping and gnashing of teeth, when ye shall see Abraham, and Isaac, and Jacob, and ALL THE PROPHETS in the kingdom of God, and you yourselves thrust out." Let us follow the JW line of reasoning here. If Abraham represents Jehovah God, and Isaac represents Christ, and Jacob the 144,000 — THEN WHOM DO ALL THE PROPHETS REPRESENT? Needless to say our errant Watchtower teacher could not answer this and so beat a hasty retreat. He that hath ears to hear let him hear. Every lie which these deceivers belch forth will only make the flames of Hell that much hotter for them.

The Old Testament saints certainly had a heavenly hope because the Psalmist declares: "Thou shalt guide me with thy counsel, and afterwards receive me to glory" (Psalm 73:24). The Bible tells us concerning the Old Testament heroes of faith: "These all died in faith, not having received the promises, but having seen them afar off, and were persuaded of them, and embraced them, and confessed that they were strangers and pilgrims on the earth. But now they desire a better country, that is, AN HEAVENLY: wherefore God is not ashamed to be called their God: for He hath prepared for them a city" (Heb. 11:13, 16). This scripture clearly tells us that the Old Testament saints had a heavenly hope.

All true Christians will go to Heaven

Jesus clearly taught that all who serve Him will surely go to Heaven. These are our Saviour's own words: "If any man (not just 144,000) serve Me, let him follow Me; and where I am, there shall also my servant be" (John 12:26). This scripture plainly teaches that all true servants of Christ will one day be in Heaven with their Saviour.

In the sermon on the mount our Lord makes this announcement: "Blessed are ye, when men shall revile you, and persecute you, and shall say all manner of evil against you falsely, for my sake. Rejoice and be exceeding glad: for great is your reward IN HEAVEN" (Matt. 5:11-12). Oh, how the JW's like to apply this text to themselves. But notice what it says here. All those who are persecuted for Christ and the true gospel HAVE THEIR REWARD IN HEAVEN.

The new earth

We are often asked this question by JW's. If all the saved are going to Heaven, then who is going to live on the New Earth? The Bible does indeed teach there is to be a new heaven and a new earth (Rev. 21:1). Both will be occupied by redeemed mankind. What JW's fail to see is that in the final consummation Heaven and the New Earth *will be one!* This truth is portrayed in the following text: "That in the dispensation of the fulness of times he might GATHER TOGETHER IN ONE all things in Christ, BOTH WHICH ARE IN HEAVEN, AND WHICH ARE ON EARTH" (Eph. 1:10).

At the present time Heaven and earth are separated by a great gulf. But in the ages to come Heaven and the New Earth will be as one. The Apostle John tells us: "I saw the holy city, new Jerusalem, coming down from God out of heaven" (Rev. 21:2). John continues on to say, "And the city had no need of the sun, neither the moon, to shine in it: for the glory of God did lighten it, and the Lamb is the light thereof. And the nations of them which are saved shall walk in the light of it: and the kings of the earth bring their glory and honour into it" (Rev. 21:23-24).

We thus see that God brings Heaven and earth together. This will be "as the days of heaven upon the earth" (Deut. 11:21). The Bible declares, "He that overcometh shall INHERIT ALL THINGS; and I will be his God, and he shall be my son" (Rev. 21:7). Notice that the righteous who overcome INHERIT ALL THINGS. In the light of this scripture, how can the Witnesses say that the earthly class of the redeemed will be restricted from Heaven? Likewise how can they maintain that the 144,000, who inherit all things, will be restricted from the New Earth? The redeemed of the Lord INHERIT ALL THINGS. Those who are saved will thus inherit both Heaven and the New Earth.

It seems that JW's are so taken up with pigeon-holing God's redeemed ones that they have missed the boat. They can tell you positively just how many are going to Heaven. They can also tell you with absolute certainty that the vast majority of the saved will spend eternity — not in Heaven — but here on earth. They seem to know all about the blessings and benefits which God's Kingdom will bring to mankind. They can tell you about the time when the lion shall lie down with the lamb and a little child shall lead them. They can even tell you about that glad day when the knowledge of the Lord shall cover the earth as the waters cover the sea. But there is one thing they can't tell you! They cannot tell you how to enter into God's Kingdom. The Lord Jesus was most emphatic about what man must do to enter into God's Kingdom. Listen well to His words: "Jesus answered and said unto him, Verily, I say unto thee, Except a man be born again, he cannot *see* the kingdom of God" (John 3:3).

The JW's talk much about God's Kingdom, but unless they are born again, they will never even SEE God's Kingdom. How is one born again? One is born again by accepting Christ into his heart by faith as his Lord and Saviour. This does not mean merely giving mental assent to the claims of Christ. It means that when you believe in Christ with all your heart, then God's spirit does a work of saving grace in your heart. When this happens one knows that he has had a personal encounter with Christ. Remember Jesus' words: "At that day YE SHALL KNOW that I am in my Father, and ye in me, and I in you" (John 14:20). Our Saviour also said, "I am the good shepherd, and know my sheep, AND AM KNOWN OF MINE" (The marginal reference literally reads: 'mine own know Me') (John 10:14).

The Bible further tells us: "He that believeth on the Son of God HATH THE WITNESS IN HIMSELF" (1 John 5:10).

The scriptures thus teach that one who truly belongs to Christ knows it. One can obtain such assurance only through the New Birth. This is the only way man can ever enter into God's Kingdom. From our study we can see that the Society has robbed the Witnesses of their right to this Biblical experience called the New Birth. Since the JW's refuse to seek this experience for themselves, they will remain eternally lost regardless of how much they talk about God's Kingdom. The words of our Saviour still hold true: "Ye must be born again."

Chapter fifteen

JEHOVAH'S WITNESSES AND THE BIBLE

The Witnesses make a great show of claiming to believe the Bible. But what is the real truth? The unvarnished truth is that JW's do not believe the Bible AS IT IS WRITTEN. They believe only the Watchtower's interpretation of the Bible. We have seen throughout this book that a great many passages of scripture flatly contradict their teachings. This does not bother the devotees of the Watchtower cult, for they will twist and wrest such scriptures to suit their own heretical views. They are most adept at glibly bending the truth of scripture to suit Watchtower doctrinal specifications. In most instances it turns out to be an exercise in futility trying to untangle a JW's mesh mash of scripture juggling. As witnesses for Christ we must ever be cognizant of the fact that an enemy has captured their minds and souls. So great and terrible is their delusion that many of them sincerely believe they have the truth regardless of all the evidence to the contrary. May God help us to deliver many from the clutches of this deceptive system.

The Witnesses are not allowed to let the Bible speak for itself. We substantiate this charge by quoting the Watchtower of May 1, 1957, p. 273:

> "Jehovah God has provided his holy written Word for all mankind and it contains all the information that is needed for men in taking a course leading to life. But God has not arranged for that Word to speak independently OR TO SHINE FORTH LIFE-GIVING TRUTHS BY ITSELF. His Word says: 'Light is sown for the righteous.' (Psa. 97:11). It is THROUGH HIS ORGANIZATION THAT GOD PROVIDES THIS LIGHT that the prophet says is the

teaching or law of the mother. If we walk in the light of
truth we must recognize not only Jehovah God as our
Father but his organization as our mother" (emphasis ours).

Do you see what they say here? They have the gall to tell us that
God's Word cannot "SHINE FORTH LIFE-GIVING TRUTHS BY ITSELF."
This proves what we have just said. The Bible by itself is not the
"truth" for JW's. It is only the Society's interpretation of the Bible
that is the "truth." We would like to ask the Witnesses this question.
Who was it that gave your Society the exclusive right to be the sole
interpreter of God's Holy Word? Could it be that the Society presumptuously took this role upon themselves? How convenient! This
assumed authority enables the Society to deceive people into believing that Jehovah is the author of their destructive heresies. The
evidence submitted in these pages proves that their dictatorial puffing
here is nothing but a hollow mockery. The facts clearly reveal that
their system of professed light is in reality the deepest kind of
spiritual darkness.

The voice of the Watchtower Society is as the voice of God to a
JW. When the Society issues a statement all Witnesses are expected to
believe it. Here is further proof about what the Society really thinks
of the Bible:

"Thus the Bible is an organizational book and belongs
to the Christian congregation as an organization, not to
individuals, regardless of how sincerely they may believe
that they can interpret the Bible. For this reason THE
BIBLE CANNOT BE PROPERLY UNDERSTOOD WITHOUT
JEHOVAH'S VISIBLE ORGANIZATION IN MIND" (emphasis
ours). Watchtower of Oct. 1, 1967, p. 587.

There you have it! Individual JW's are thus forbidden by the
Society to interpret the Bible for themselves. The Society has decreed
that it will do all spiritual thinking for them. The Watchtower
hierarchy of today is merely echoing here what Pastor Russell said
when he was alive:

"Furthermore, not only do we find that people cannot see the divine plan in studying the Bible by itself, but
we see, also, that if anyone lays the 'Scripture Studies'

(Russell's writings) aside, even after he has used them, after he has read them for ten years . . . if he then lays them aside and ignores them and goes to the Bible alone, though he has understood his Bible for ten years, our experience shows THAT WITHIN TWO YEARS HE GOES INTO DARKNESS" (emphasis ours). Watchtower of Sept. 15, 1910, p. 298.

Just think of it! To read the Bible alone without the writings of this strutting Watchtower egotist IS TO WALK IN DARKNESS ! ! ! As we have just seen, the Watchtower Society of today still holds this same arrogant attitude. This is the sort of lying propaganda which keeps JW's on a steady diet of Watchtower study aids.

The Watchtower hierarchy has usurped the position of teacher and guide which rightfully belongs only to the Holy Spirit. This cult has deceived vast numbers of people with the lie that their Society is Jehovah's only teacher and guide for man today. Nothing could be further from the truth. It is true that God does use human instruments to teach and preach His Word. But no man or Society has any right to proclaim (as the JW's do) that God deals only through them. If JW's would study the Bible without Watchtower aids, they would soon see through many of the Society's erroneous interpretations of scripture.

Regardless of what the Watchtower proclaims, every person does have the God-given right to read and to interpret the Bible for himself. Proof for this is seen in the fact that Christ invites all men to "Search the scriptures" (John 5:39). We also read about the Bereans who "searched the scriptures daily" to see whether the things they heard were true (Acts 17:11). The Apostle John speaking to Spirit filled Christians declares: "Ye need not that any man teach you" (1 John 2:27). The Christian's guide and teacher then is not man — certainly not the Watchtower Society — but the Holy Spirit. Christ made this very clear when He said, "But the Comforter which is the Holy Ghost . . . HE SHALL TEACH YOU ALL THINGS" (John 14:26).

The JW's will try to justify their position by saying that the eunuch in Acts 8:26 could not understand the scriptures until Philip explained them to him. The parallel is then made by JW's that men today likewise cannot understand the Bible either unless it is explained to them. This seems like a valid point. However upon examination we find that the reason the eunuch did not understand the prophecy in Isaiah from which he was reading was because HE DID NOT HAVE THE NEW TESTAMENT TO GUIDE HIM. It had not yet been written. The New Testament explains the Old Testament. Thus the problem which the eunuch had does not present itself today. The arrogant dogmatism of the Watchtower claim that only the Society has the sole right to interpret God's Word is thus shown to be not only presumptuous but also scripturally repugnant.

Another argument put forth by the Witnesses in this connection is that no man has any right to privately interpret the Bible for himself. To try and prove this they will quote 2 Peter 1:20 — "Knowing this first, that no prophecy of the scripture is of any private interpretation." If this text means what the JW's maintain, then what right did Russell and Rutherford have to PRIVATELY interpret the Bible for their followers? Also what right do the present day leaders of the Watchtower Movement have to PRIVATELY interpret the Bible for JW's?

One of the great principles of the Protestant Reformation is the right of every believer to interpret or understand the scriptures for himself. Certainly our text here does not condemn this principle. Rather it is telling us "that no PROPHECY of the scripture is of any private interpretation." Notice what this text says here — it is talking about "prophecy." In other words man is not to put his own fanciful interpretation upon the PROPHETIC WORD. We agree that in the broad sense our text also teaches that one is not to privately interpret a verse of scripture by itself. We must consider the verse in question within its context. It has been well said that a text taken out of context is a pretext. The testimony of scripture is that God invites everyone to read His Holy Word. Our Lord has graciously given the Holy Spirit, the Christian's teacher and guide, to personally speak to each heart concerning Bible truth.

They pose as defenders of the Bible

The JW's have recently added a new gimmick to their sales pitch.

They are now posing as defenders of the Holy Bible and have gone on record to sanctimoniously deplore the apostate condition of certain Churches in Christendom. The Witnesses are at their crafty best in an article entitled: "Parents What Are Your Children Being Taught" (Awake, Feb. 22, 1967). In this particular article the JW's criticize the United Church of Canada for denying the miracles of the Bible. Parents are urged in this Awake magazine ". . . to look somewhere other than to such churches of Christendom for help in teaching your children about God and the Bible. Standing ready to help you are the Christian witnesses of Jehovah in your community." Well, isn't this nice of the JW's to be so concerned for the spiritual welfare of Sunday School children! These deceivers certainly don't miss a trick. The real meaning behind this gracious JW invitation is that parents should try their brand of spiritual poison!

In the Awake magazine of April 22, 1969, the JW's launched a massive all-out attack against the Churches of Christendom. This particular issue of the Awake was taken up solely with slam-banging all the Churches. One article in this Awake magazine was entitled: "DO THE CHURCHES UPHOLD BIBLE TEACHINGS" (p. 10). This article listed several quotations made by certain apostate Methodist, Episcopal, Lutheran and Catholic clergymen who favoured *fornication, adultery and homosexuality*. The author of the Awake article then made this conclusion:

> "What does such an examination indicate? Would you say that these Catholic and Protestant churches uphold the teachings of the Bible? Do they endeavor to follow closely what God says in his Word? Obviously they do not. The belief that all teachings of the churches are based upon the Bible is a complete misconception. And now these churches are making clear their tremendous apostasy by condoning immorality, including fornication, adultery, and even homosexuality" (page 14).

No informed Bible believing Christian denies that there are apostate clergymen within the liberal camp of Christendom. But this cannot be said of the great Evangelical Churches of Christendom. The Evangelicals (born again Christians) certainly do not condone immorality, such as fornication, adultery, and homosexuality. In fact Evangelicals strongly preach against such practises. Neither do Evangelicals deny the miracles of the Bible or the authority of Holy Scripture. The authors of the Awake magazine knew all this, but they deliberately avoided mentioning it. The way out statements made by certain apostate clergymen are used to full advantage by JW's to smear the Churches. The Awake magazine did not tell the whole truth concerning this matter. The articles were deliberately slanted to create the impression that all the Churches were apostate and therefore not of God. Such unfair reporting reveals their ingrained prejudice against the true Church of Jesus Christ.

We do not hesitate to boldly announce that Jehovah's Witnesses are worse than the apostate clergymen whom they have just denounced. Of all the religious deceivers which plague mankind today the Witnesses rank among the most despicable. Why? BECAUSE WATCHTOWER DECEIVERS DELIBERATELY WREST THE HOLY SCRIPTURES IN ORDER TO DECEIVE PEOPLE. Other false prophets such as Christian Scientists, Mormons, Spiritualists, Liberals and Modernists also deceive people. However, these deceivers are more honest than the JW's (if that is possible), for they at least tell their intended victims that they do not abide solely by Holy Scripture. We only wish the JW's were at least that honest.

Even such militant infidels as Voltaire, Thomas Payne, and Robert Ingersoll were more honest and above board than the JW's. These God haters at least put their cards on the table and openly admitted to the people that they did not believe the Bible. The JW's, however, are a different breed of false prophet. They prefer to deceive people by twisting and perverting the Holy Scriptures.

Trapping their victim

Unsuspecting people are lured into the Watchtower cult by those who have been trained in the art of subterfuge and evasion. The JW is well aware that the average householder knows very little about the Bible. This lack of Bible knowledge, on the part of the householder, enables the JW to proceed in his sales pitch without being contradicted.

The typical JW is confident that he can have things his own way with one who does not know the Bible. Attempting to be ever so gracious, the JW will smilingly try to "soft sell" his heretical wares whenever possible. The uninformed householder is certainly no match for these well trained salesmen from Heresy Inc.

On first contacting a potential convert, the JW deceiver will pose as "an angel of light." He will even speak forth some truth! (This is done to gain the intended victim's confidence.) With simpering sweetness and a smile of insincerity our JW salesman will open the Bible and show the interested householder what wonderful blessings there will be during the Millennium! With righteous indignation he will also denounce the evils of war and the falsity of evolution! The sad spiritual decline of many LIBERAL Churches likewise brings forth sympathetic comments. (The JW will carefully omit the word "LIBERAL" here so as to create the impression that all the Churches are now apostate.)

The sincere householder is quite impressed with what he has heard thus far. The Watchtower salesman then suggests they get together next week to further discuss the Bible. Not wishing to offend such a knowledgeable and seemingly pleasant person, the householder gives his consent. Thus the thin edge of the wedge is in and the groundwork has been laid.

The back call

The following week our well-dressed polite JW salesman returns as scheduled. During the evening's discussion the Church is criticized (ever so slightly at first) for allowing the world to get into such a terrible state. (Since when are the evil conditions of this world the fault of the Church?) Criticism of historic Christianity becomes more pronounced with each passing study period. With barbed words of scornful disdain the JW teacher begins to OPENLY RIDICULE THE FAITH OF OUR FOUNDING FATHERS. The arrogant dogmatism of the Watchtower's man-made perversions is slowly substituted for the great doctrines of historic Christianity. Hell is laughed out the window. The Holy Trinity is blasphemed and ridiculed. Christ is openly robbed of His Deity and reduced from His position as Lord and God to that of a mere creature. Even worship to Christ is branded as sacrilegious. The great truth of Christ's Bodily Resurrection is also denied by these deceivers. By performing word gymnastics they can even make out that the Second Coming of Christ took place INVISIBLY in 1914!

The JW who first appeared at our unsuspecting householder's door months before, claiming to be of God, now reveals by his doctrine that he is indeed a false prophet. The deceptive lying spirit which drives him from house to house now begins to stir and to show itself. Week by week and month after month our bewildered householder friend is constantly subjected to a barrage of Watchtower propaganda. The victim's mind begins to reel and stagger under the great weight of lies, half-truths and false reasonings. The last strands of resistance are finally broken down and the mind capitulates. This is conversion — Watchtower style! Oh, the souls that have been damned by such brainwashing tactics. Oh, the cunning and shrewd way in which victims are lured into this soul-destroying delusion.

Victims of deception

Within this book we have probed the complexities of Watchtower heretical thinking. The many glaring weaknesses in their doctrinal structure have been pointed out and exposed. The evidence clearly shows that the doctrines of this cult are grievous errors woven from the dark recesses of unregenerate minds. Throughout these pages Reason and Truth have cried aloud to stop them, but being deceived they will not listen. Their ears are deaf to the voice of God in scripture. Bright pictures of false reasoning have so dazzled them that truth becomes a lie and a lie becomes the truth. It is even as the Apostle Paul has stated:

> "But if our gospel be hid, it is hid to them that are lost: In whom the god of this world hath blinded the minds of them which believe not, lest the light of the glorious gospel of Christ, who is the image of God, should shine unto them" (2 Cor. 4:3-4).

The Witnesses have an educated ignorance of the Word of God. Those ensnared by this cult have grown so accustomed to their own unreason that they have lost the power of astonishment. The constant drilling of destructive heresies into their minds has given them a twisted concept of spiritual things. The drumbeat of verbal and written opiate has finally deadened the senses of these poor blinded creatures. Caught up as they are in their own perverse logic, it is, in most cases, virtually impossible to reason with them. Within this book we have answered their treason against the great truths of historic Christianity. Our study has revealed that Watchtower error can only flourish where there is ignorance of God's Word.

You will recall that in the beginning of this book the statement was made that we would venture into the dark caverns of heretical thought — not just to curse the darkness — but to search for those who were deceived by a false gospel. Surely it has been amply demonstrated that the doctrinal position of the Watchtower Society is indeed false. We would be remiss in our Christian duty not to point the way out of this spiritual darkness and confusion. There is hope even for those who are bound and shackled with doctrinal Watchtower chains. That hope is in Christ who came to set the captive free.

As we near the end of this book, I pray that God will burn upon every heart the solemn fact: "It is appointed unto men once to die, but after this the judgment" (Heb. 9:27). When the dark shadow of approaching death begins to steal across your path — what then? We are all fellow travelers to the bar of God. As a JW you have put your faith and trust in an organization called the Watchtower Society. What has it done for you? Has the Society taught you to seek a personal experience with Christ? No! Instead they have given you knowledge. But we have seen in this book that the knowledge they have instilled into you is not the truth. It is false. The wisdom they have taught you "descendeth not from above, but is earthly, sensual, DEVILISH" (James 3:15).

Chapter sixteen

THE ONE CHANNEL

The JW's maintain that man cannot approach God on his own. According to them all of God's dealings with man today are done through only one channel — the Watchtower Society. This is not a new idea; other false cults also make the same claim. We do not for a moment deny that God does deal with man through only one channel. But who is this one channel? It is none other than Christ Himself. Holy Writ tells us that there is only "one mediator between God and men, the man Christ Jesus" (1 Tim. 2:5). We thus see that Christ is the only mediator (or channel) men need come to when seeking God. Christ Himself said, with authority: "I am the Way, the Truth, and the Life, no man cometh unto the Father but by Me" (John 14:6). This same truth is reiterated in Acts 4:12 — "Neither is there salvation in any other: for there is none other name under Heaven given among men, whereby we must be saved." In the light of such scriptures, how can the Watchtower Society presumptuously claim an exclusive monopoly on man's access to God?

Taking in knowledge

The JW's are quick to quote John 17:3 when the matter of man's salvation is mentioned: "This means everlasting life, the taking in knowledge of you, the only true God and of the one whom you sent forth, Jesus Christ" (JW Bible). The Witnesses believe this text teaches that everlasting life comes by taking in knowledge. They tell us that knowledge can only be taken in by study and learning. Hence the reason for their many magazines and books and the long hours they spend in studying them. What is it they learn in their books? They learn what the Society wants them to learn — namely to loathe, hate and despise the cardinal beliefs of historic Christianity. They learn to deride and ridicule those who tell the old, old story of Jesus and His love. This is what they piously call "taking in knowledge."

The term *"taking in knowledge"* in John 17:3 is found only in the JW version of the Bible. The Witnesses have obviously translated it this way to try and get people to believe that everlasting life comes only by the way of acquiring knowledge. All other versions of the Bible have only the following reading or something akin to it: "And this is life eternal, that they might know thee the only true God, and Jesus Christ, whom thou hast sent" (John 17:3). Notice here that eternal life comes by KNOWING God. This denotes a personal relationship between the believer and God. There is a considerable difference between KNOWING God and in merely having knowledge about God. The Pharisees had a knowledge about God, even as do the JW's today, BUT THEY DID NOT KNOW GOD. This is made obvious by the fact that Christ said unto them: "Ye neither KNOW me nor my Father" (John 8:19).

Let us consider this text: "He that entereth not by the door (Christ) but climbeth up some other way (the way of knowledge), the same is a thief and a robber" (John 10:1). The JW's come under the scathing rebuke of Christ here and are denounced by Him as thieves and robbers because they are proclaiming that man can come to God by another way, by the way of the mere taking in of knowledge — Watchtower kind! The whole tenor of scripture bears out the fact that "the world by wisdom knew not God" (1 Cor. 1:21). Paul goes on to say, "the Greeks seek after wisdom: but we preach Christ crucified" (1 Cor. 1:21-22). It is this fact — that Christ was crucified — which is "the power of God AND THE WISDOM OF GOD" (1 Cor. 1:23-24). If the JW's really want people to take in the wisdom of God, then why do they not preach and emphasize what Paul declared was truly the power of God and the wisdom of God — CHRIST CRUCIFIED.

Paul further states that he "came not with excellency of speech or of wisdom. For I determined not to know anything among you, SAVE JESUS CHRIST AND HIM CRUCIFIED" (1 Cor. 2:1-2). The Witnesses will admit that Paul truly preached the gospel. What was it that Paul preached? Did he preach that wisdom was the gospel? No! Paul declares that the gospel is JESUS CHRIST AND HIM CRUCIFIED. Who today is preaching Jesus Christ and Him crucified? Are the JW's taken up with preaching and emphasizing this great truth? No! They claim this is old stuff and that everyone knows about it. They are more interested in preaching their so-called new light. The born again Christians are the ones who are preaching to a lost and dying world JESUS CHRIST AND HIM CRUCIFIED. Thus it is established beyond doubt that the born again Christians are the ones truly preaching the gospel and not the JW's. The Watchtower gospel is not the gospel Paul preached. The gospel of the Watchtower is a soul destroying gospel, and those who have accepted it have taken a consuming curse into their bosoms.

Mere intellectual knowledge about God and the Bible is not enough. Knowledge tends to make the unregenerate heart of man proud and haughty. The Bible declares as much in these words: "Knowledge puffeth up, but love edifieth" (1 Cor. 8:1). The love spoken of here that edifies is "the love of God shed abroad in our hearts by the Holy Ghost" (Rom. 5:5). This love is given by the Holy Spirit at the time of conversion when the sinful heart is changed and the soul is born again. It is this divine love that makes the believer love the unlovely. It is this love that drives the believer to his knees to ask God with cryings and tears to save the souls of those lost in sin and error. JW's know nothing of the burden of such interceding prayer. They know nothing of the "weeping that may endure for a night, or of the joy that cometh in the morning" (Psalm 30:5). They know nothing about the peace of God that passes all understanding. Nor do they know anything about the joy of sins forgiven; that joy which is indeed inexpressible and full of glory. They do not know, nor can they sing, the song of the soul set free. Neither do these who have accepted this delusion know anything about "the love of Christ WHICH PASSETH KNOWLEDGE" (Eph. 3:19).

The JW's always appear to be in a strained condition; forever trying to prove or disprove something. Their religion is one of argumentation, forever trying to conjure up new ideas and new theories to bolster their tissue of falsehoods. Many of these poor benighted souls have become so deeply enmeshed in this heresy that it is virtually impossible to reason with them. Their so-called superior Watchtower knowledge has had an adverse effect on their personalities. It has made many of them proud, arrogant and puffed up. Most of these people have no love in their hearts for those who would dare disagree with them. There are those among them who look at you with fierce fiery eyes of hate and contempt when you tell them that they need to repent and get right with God. These are a people who indeed "are ever learning, and never able to come to the knowledge of the truth" (2 Tim. 3:7).

Salvation found only in Christ

The following wonderful promise is given unto us by Christ: "Come unto Me, all ye that labour and are heavy laden, and I will give you rest" (Matt. 11:28). Notice that we are all lovingly invited to come. But to whom are we to come? The Watchtower Society? Some other cult? Perhaps even the Church! No, we are to come directly to the Lord Jesus Christ, for it is only He who can give the weary soul rest. But how are we to come? We are to come to Christ with the simplicity of little children. Remember Jesus saying, "Except ye be converted and become as little children, ye shall not enter the kingdom of heaven" (Matt. 18:3). A little child is one who has simple faith and loving trust. The seeking soul must come to God displaying these characteristics. Man must humble himself AS A LITTLE CHILD if he is to find God. He must bow before God and in a childlike way pour out his heart to Him. Ofttimes because of deep Godly sorrow for sins committed, there will be strong cryings and tears from the penitent one. At this time of humble contrition, the penitent soul promises to forsake his sins and to accept Christ as his Lord and Saviour. When this state of total surrender to Christ is reached, then the sweet peace and presence of God begins to permeate and flood the soul. Joy unspeakable and full of glory now becomes his portion. A new name is written down in Heaven, and the angels rejoice because another sinner has repented and found the Saviour.

The JW's have nothing but contempt and ridicule for those who preach this kind of a gospel. Their vitriolic scorn and scoffer's venom will, however, only loom up before them in eternity to mock their lost souls. For unless they repent and accept God's way of salvation, they will be cast down into the darkness and horrors of eternal night. This will be a place of weeping, wailing and gnashing of teeth. This is that dreadful place where only the rolling thunder of Hell's eternal cry is ever heard amid the blackness of darkness forever (Matt. 25:30-41). Repent, for why will ye perish?

The Witnesses are so deceived they believe that the kind of repentance preached by born again Christians is not truly Bible repentance at all, but rather is extreme fanaticism and of the devil. O the depths of deception! The pride of the JW screams out in protest against the kind of Bible repentance that would so humble him in the dust that the glory of his sinful pride would be shorn. They forget that it is written: "He that shall humble himself shall be exalted" (Matt. 23:12). The Witnesses think they can come to God their way. The road they have chosen is the way of the flesh. There is no deep thorough humbling and abasement of self. There is no loathing and abhorrence of sin among them. They have no assurance that all is right between their soul and the Saviour. They are forever tramping from house to house telling people how right they are and how wrong everyone else is. These people have never personally settled the sin question, for if they had then they would be serving the Christ of Heaven instead of the Watchtower Society of Brooklyn, N.Y.

All those who come weeping their way through to God are labelled by the JW's as fanatical and emotional. They forget that it is written: "God now commandeth all men everywhere to repent" (Acts 17:30). When Peter denied Jesus three times he "went out and wept bitterly" (Luke 22:62). Paul speaks of serving the Lord with many tears (Acts 20:19). David utters a beautiful truth when he says, "They that sow in tears shall reap in joy" (Psalm 126:5). Godly sorrow and repentance then are interwoven; you cannot separate them. It is therefore entirely natural and scriptural for a sinner to shed tears of sorrow for sin when he comes to Christ. One wonders if the JW's are able to shed tears of sorrow for their sins? If not — why not?

Those of the Watchtower persuasion know nothing about the deeper depths and higher heights in Christ. They do not know what it is to worship the Lord in the Spirit. They do not know the blessing of lingering at the feet of Jesus in prayer. Their souls have never felt the intimacy of Christ's divine love. They have never in prayer had a revelation or an unveiling of God's great heart of love. O that the JW's would lay aside their Watchtower and begin to seek the Christ for sinners slain.

The Witnesses do not believe that a sinner can become reconciled to God in a moment of time. They think it is wrong and presumptuous for a man to say that he is now saved and justified by the grace of God. But what saith the scriptures? Jesus tells us of a man who went into the temple to pray, and who smote his breast and cried: "God be merciful to me a sinner." Jesus answered: "I tell you, this man went down to his house justified" (Luke 18:13-14). How did this sinner become reconciled to God? By his good works? No! He found forgiveness and was justified, or saved, not by any good thing he had done; but rather by humbling himself and crying unto God in prayer to have mercy on him. Dear reader, you too can be saved from your sins and make Heaven your home if you will but cry unto Jesus to save you. O soul sinking down 'neath life's pitiless waves, the strong arm of Jesus is mighty to save.

Scripture Index

To list all the verses in this essay would make our Index too voluminous. Therefore only those passages more particularly discussed will be noted.